BRITISH GRASSES, SEDGES & RUSHES

BRITISH GRASSES, SEDGES & RUSHES

BRITISH GRA...

BRITISH GRAS...

GRASSES...

& RUSHES

& RUSHES

& RUSHES

7   7   7   7   7

THE OBSERVER'S BOOK OF

THE OBSERVER'S BOOK OF

DOGS

CW00695603

HORSES & PONIES

HORSES & PONIES

9   9

The Observer's Book of BRITISH GEOLOGY

The Observer's Book of BRITISH GEOLOGY

The Observer's Book of BRITISH GEOLOGY

The Observer's Book of BRITISH GEOLOGY

The Observer's Book of BRITISH GEOLOGY

The Observer's Book of BRITISH GEOLOGY

GEOLOGY

GEOLOGY

GEOLOGY

10   10   10   10   10   10   10   10

The Observer's Book of

OBSERVER'S BOOKS

The Observer's Book of
BUTTERFLIES

154 ILLUSTRATIONS
IN COLOUR and BLACK & WHITE
ALL SPECIES DESCRIBED

THE OBSERVER'S BOOK OF
HORSES & PONIES

by R. S. SUMMERHAYS
60 ILLUSTRATIONS
90 BREEDS DESCRIBED

The Observer's Book
of BRITISH
WILD ANIMALS

72 ILLUSTRATIONS
IN COLOUR and BLACK & WHITE
69 SPECIES DESCRIBED

The Observer's Book of
TREES & SHRUBS
OF THE BRITISH ISLES

177 ILLUSTRATIONS
IN COLOUR and BLACK & WHITE
106 SPECIES DESCRIBED

The Observer's Book of
SILVER

ELIZABETH DE CASTRES

The Observer's Book of
CRICKET

PETER SMITH

The Observer's Book of
OLD ENGLISH CHURCHES

LAWRENCE E. JONES

The Observer's Book of
GARDEN FLOWERS

200 SPECIES DESCRIBED
ALL FULLY ILLUSTRATED
IN COLOUR and BLACK & WHITE

The Observer's Book of

OBSERVER'S BOOKS

PETER MARREN and JOHN CARTER

WITH 8 COLOUR PLATES
BY MICHAEL J. AMPHLETT
AND 80 HALF-TONES,
MAINLY BY THE AUTHORS

PEREGRINE BOOKS
LEEDS

First published in 1999
by Peregrine Books by permission of
Frederick Warne & Co.

27 Hunger Hills Avenue, Horsforth
Leeds LS18 5JS

We dedicate this book to the memory of
A.F. Stuart 1912-1995
who designed the Observer's Books and
John Clegg 1909-1998
natural history advisor to Frederick Warne
and author of *The Observer's Book of Pond Life*

The endpapers show part of a collection
of every printing of Observer's books.
The front endpaper is of books published
in the 1950s and 1960s; the back endpaper
in the late 1970s and early 1980s.

ISBN 0 9520268 5 6

Printed and bound in Great Britain by
SMITH SETTLE
Ilkley Road, Otley
West Yorkshire LS21 3JP

The Observer's Pocket Series 1937-1982

Details of titles, authors, editions and illustrators are found in Part 4: Bibliography. The full title of each book is 'The Observer's Book of ....', here abbreviated to the subject.

and the obligatory whiskers, gazing directly and steadily at the viewer with an inquiring air. He radiates the confidence of the self-made man, his evident sense of his own worth relieved by a humorous twinkle. He looks tough, but paternal, rather like a kindly chimpanzee, with his broad, thin-lipped mouth, deep eyes and hairless forehead. He had a way with him. Frederick Warne habitually called his office boys 'Mister', his male servants 'John', and his women servants 'Mary', irrespective of their real names. He insisted on formal dress – frock coats, striped trousers and top hats – for his staff, and that went for trips to the country as well as in the office. Despite such eccentricities, or perhaps because of them, he built up a core of loyal staff who remained with the firm throughout their careers, as did their descendants as late as the 1960s. In his spare time Warne enjoyed carriage-rides and fishing for perch at Slapton Ley in Devon. He enjoyed company, indulged in jovial luncheon parties at his well-appointed home in Bedford Square, and was fond of whist and cribbage.

In 1865, the partnership of Frederick Warne and George Routledge was dissolved 'by mutual consent'. Warne decided to strike out on his own, and found business premises at Bedford Street, Covent Garden, an area described as 'a strange mixture of fruit and publishing'. Warne's motto was 'healthy literature at popular prices'. One means of achieving this was the publication of popular series of books. Warne was among the first publishers to cater for the mass market, as working class literacy increased through proper schooling and methods of machine printing steadily improved. A lot of Warne's early productions were aimed at children, both cheap editions of classics and moral tracts for 'Working and Cottage Homes' with titles like 'My Duties; or Why was I made?'. In 1902, Warne became the publisher of Beatrix Potter's stories. Perhaps its established blend of natural history and story books for the young made Warne an attractive choice (though Beatrix was to become engaged to one of the Warnes). Most of Potter's stories were published in white wrappers and a short square format suited to a young child. Moreover, Potter's delicate coloured drawings had to be printed on pure white coated paper, suitable for fine reproduction. Both ideas were to influence the design of the Observer's series, 30 years later.

There are further echoes of the Observer's books in an early Warne venture, the 'Popular Natural History' library, 24 cloth-bound seven-and-sixpenny titles, including Popular British Ornithology (by Philip Gosse, no less), British Birds' Eggs, History of British Ferns, History of British Mosses and Popular Physical Geology. A review in The Standard praised this 'popular series of scientific treatises, which, from the simplicity of their style, and the artistic excellences and correctness of their numerous illustrations, has acquired a celebrity beyond that of any other series of modern cheap works'.

In 1895, Frederick Warne retired, leaving the firm in the hands of his three sons. In that year, they published a small crimson book by a 40-year-old nature writer, Edward Step, called Wayside and Woodland Blossoms. It was the first title of what was to become a long-running and famous series, the Wayside and Woodland Books, designed for the observant wayfarer. They were the forerunners of the presentday field guides, and were designed to fit the pocket. These books were revolutionary. A pocket book needed to be short, concise, well-illustrated and accurate. It had to be made suitable for the beginner, and every bird, insect or flower described needed a clearly printed and lifelike corresponding picture, preferably in colour. Edward Step

Edward Step (1855-1931).

knew instinctively what was needed from his close involvement with wild life societies and rambling groups. Few at that time could have matched his all-round knowledge and grasp, nor the clarity of his prose, nor his ability to tell a story without reducing wild animals to little people or wild flowers to sterile decorative objects.

Edward Step was the real author of most of the early titles in the Observer's series, though, like Frederick Warne, he did not live long enough to see even the first book. This is because the texts he wrote for the Wayside and Woodland volumes on trees, wild animals and ferns were later plundered, more or less verbatim, for their corresponding Observer's titles (see below). *The Observer's Book of Butterflies* was an equally recycled text, based on the classic *Wayside and Woodland Butterflies* by Richard South, written in 1906. This does not mean that the first Observer's Books were out of date, for such basic information does not date quickly. But it did mean that Frederick Warne & Co could cut costs by recycling text and pictures already in their copyright, and, in the latter case, using printing blocks already available. That is one reason why the books were so inexpensive, and why Warne could produce them and their competitors could not.

A more immediate factor behind the Observer's series

was the advent of cheap illustrated libraries in the 1930s. More or less contemporary with the first Observer's books were Allen Lane's King Penguins – pocket-sized, hardback, all-colour books specialising in natural history and collecting. The first of them was *British Birds* (1937) illustrated with ancient colour prints by John Gould. A few years later, the same publisher's Puffin Picture series for the young began, similar

A Wayside and Woodland title in a 1950s jacket.

to the Observer's in spirit, but with flimsy paper covers. A similar idea inspired the half-crown *Britain in Pictures*, published by Collins and Adprint as 'a series of illustrated essays on British culture and achievements' and, once again, the first (and most successful) title in this series was about birds. The moral seemed to be: if you want to start with a bang, begin with Birds (and, in the 1940s at least, it was also a good idea to put 'British' in the title). It was against this background – natural history, advances in colour printing, the cheap popular series and the competitiveness between publishing houses in these fields – that the idea for an Observer's Pocket Series emerged.

Mr Scott and Mr Stokoe have lunch

In June 1937, Frederick Warne & Co Ltd – it had become a limited company in 1920 – published the first two titles of the new Observer's Pocket Series: *British Birds* and *British*

Wild Flowers. Each was remarkable for its unusual size (5³/₄ x 3⁵/₈ inches) and low price – half a crown (2/6 or 12¹/₂p) – or 2/9 (14p) by post. They were 'handy' in the literal sense of fitting one's hand, and so suitable for taking with you on country walks and cycle rides; they presented a novel integration of text and pictures; the colour pictures were lavish and of high quality; and most remarkable of all was the astounding price. Half-crown pictorial nature books were normally written for young children, and were of no use to the serious naturalist. But these books were 'grown up' field guides presenting the type of information normally found in large tomes costing a guinea or more.

The purpose of these new pocket field guides was summed up by Warne on the flyleaf of the book:

> There has long been a call for a series of Nature books, published at a *popular price*, suitable for carrying in the pocket, giving accurate illustrations so that the reader can quickly recognise the natural objects met with during a walk in the country.

The publishers believe they have met this requirement

The first two Observer's Books, published in spring 1937.

with the beautiful plates and short but interesting text found in this series.

This *raison d'être* is echoed by the author of *The Observer's Book of Birds*, Miss S. Vere Benson:

> For many years I have, from time to time, been asked by birdlovers to recommend a really inexpensive pocket textbook of British birds. Usually I could recommend nothing that was not either too bulky, too expensive or inadequate to the needs of the would-be ornithologist.

> I think no one will be able to say that this one is either too large or too expensive, or that it is inadequately illustrated.

As we have seen, the reason why these books cost only 12 1/2p was that Frederick Warne did not need to spend money on rights, royalties and new technology. The books used the same publishing materials that produced Beatrix Potter and the Wayside and Woodland books. In the case of OB *Birds*, Warne owned the copyright of the best bird pictures then available – they had purchased them back in 1925 for *Wayside and Woodland Birds* by T.A. Coward, and had the blocks ready. As a bookseller remarked, 'you know, Warne get more value out of their plates than any other house I know'. In the mid-1930s, that time of deep recession when people were strapped for cash, Warne had decided to produce cheap abridged versions of some of its nature titles. This became the task of two long-serving editors on the verge of retirement, T.H. Scott and William J. Stokoe. According to *The House of Warne* (1965), these two were close friends and used to lunch together regularly:

Mr Stokoe was a bearded and dignified gentleman

[he is said to have resembled the King, George V].
He would descend the stairs at one o'clock and knock
on Mr Scott's door and await his appearance. They
would then solemnly walk off to lunch without, so
far as one ever knew, a word being exchanged between them, either coming or going.

No doubt when they did talk, they talked about books.
In 1936, Scott and Stokoe compiled 'Wild Flowers of the
Wayside and Woodland' based on Edward Step's 3-volume
Wayside and Woodland Blossoms. In the same year they
prepared 'Birds of the Wayside and Woodland', with help
from the youthful Enid Blyton (who contributed a well-written and surprisingly grown-up introduction). Two years
later Stokoe added a third book to the list, Butterflies and

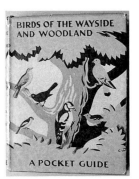

Moths of the Wayside and
Woodland, based on the
original volumes by Richard
South. It was no coincidence
that birds, wild flowers and
butterflies are the first three
books in the Observer's
Pocket Series. They were all
part of a boiling down of
stock nature books to cater
for the market for mass-produced cheap editions in
the 1930s.

The job could easily have
been done hastily and badly,
in which case we would
never have heard of *The
Observer's Book of Birds*.

The boiled-down Wayside Pocket
Guide edited by Enid Blyton,
immediate forerunner of The
Observer's Book of Birds.

Fortunately the little book was a minor masterpiece. Most of the early nature titles in the series were edited by Stokoe, but in the case of this first book in the series Warne recruited the 27-year-old S. Vere Benson. When in her teens, Vere Benson had founded The Bird Lover's League which, by 1937, had pledged 30,000 people across the world to help protect wild birds by boycotting the plumage trade. She also wrote lively articles about birds for the popular press, and, in later years, became an authority on birds of the Middle East. For the Observer's book, she made the vital decision to include one bird per page, and break up the text into notes on habits, the nest, eggs, food and call notes. Within this framework, her writing is simple, clear and accurate. For example, we can note that the chaffinch lays '4 to 6 eggs, grey, tinged with pink, and with brown blotches', in a 'very neat, round nest of moss, lichens, wool, feathers and hair, well worked and felted together', and that its call-note is a crisp "pink" and a questioning "weet". Using the splendid (if indifferently printed) colour illustrations by Thorburn, you quickly track down your bird, and find the basic information on nest, call-notes and distribution on the same page. The formula worked so well that little further revision was needed for half a century. And since Vere Benson was given a small royalty on each book sold, she must have regarded those few months in 1936 as profitably spent!

But who, one wonders, thought of the series title 'Observer's'? It is more subtle than it might appear. Look at the position of that apostrophe. It is singular, a possessive prefix. The Observer in question is not just any old observer: it is *you*, the owner of the little book. (This was lost on Penguin Books who in the 1980s changed it to 'Observers' without an apostrophe which turns it into an ungrammatical brand-name.)   The word is just right for the unfolding theme of the series, based on personal observation, and, through seeing, understanding. But who was the genius that thought of it? Alas, we do not know. Possibly Warne's then managing director, Arthur L. Stephens, who would certainly have taken the key decisions. Possibly W.A. Herring, his long-standing production manager, or his then assistant, Richard Billington, an expert on illustrated children's books. Or it might have been William Stokoe, who edited and designed the first books in the series, and was himself an accomplished artist and naturalist.

We have been told that it was probably Herring and Billington who between them designed the famous Observer's jackets and decided such matters as their exact size. Herring was responsible for preparing Beatrix Potter's work for publication, including the white jackets of the Peter Rabbit books. The ornate lettering of the Observer's jackets is said to be based on Potter's own lettering. Warne was a very 'hands-on' firm in those days, and it seems to have been Herring himself who drew the early artwork, including the fiddly scalloped edges of the jackets, though the task was passed, in the late 1940s, to Albert Stuart, the new art director.

The actual production of the books passed from Bill Stokoe's office to the Warne production department and thence to the firm's regular printer-binder, William Clowes & Sons of Beccles, Suffolk. The early titles were all printed on expensive surfaced paper, suitable for coloured inks. Such paper had to be fine-textured and wood-free, and coated with china clay to prevent any absorption of inks when the pictures were printed by letter-press. Even so, the task of printing the *Birds* pictures required exact colour-registering, which was barely obtainable with the technology

The typepress machine used to print the early Observer's Books, two colours at a time.

of the time – it was a tribute to the skill of the printers that it was as good as it was; in later editions it became much improved. Clowes also cut and case-bound the pages, and printed the jackets. Once production was underway, Warne advertised the books in its regular lists, and the firm's well-organised teams of travellers toured the country taking orders for the forthcoming titles. One such traveller at this time was Arthur King, who later became an editor of the series, and compiled *The Observer's Book of Garden Flowers*.

In those prewar days, the Observer's Books seem to have been conceived of as a nature series, matching their parent books in the Wayside and Woodland series. *British Birds* and *British Wild Flowers* were the two nature titles most likely to do well, and they were in practice, if not in specific intention, pilots for the whole series. They were given rather drab jackets with sketchy pen and ink drawings, and only a relatively modest 20,000 copies of each were printed. Yet they were successful and sold out within a few months. It was a more colourful quartet of books that appeared on sale in early 1938, when the newly reprinted and rejacketed *Birds* and *Wild Flowers* were joined by *British Butterflies* and *Trees and Shrubs*, and, later on that year, by a fifth title, *British Wild Animals* (at this stage the books were not numbered). The titles were reasonably, if not yet spectacularly successful, and by 1940 some 200,000 copies had been sold. Other titles were on the stocks, planned at the rate of two per year – one in spring and the other in autumn. Warne seemed to have a modest success on its hands. Then Germany invaded Poland, and war broke out.

Bombs and rationing

The first bombshell to hit the series in 1940 was a price rise from 2/6 to 3 shillings, 'to cover war costs'. A more serious blow was the introduction of paper rationing in 1940. Like other publishers, Warne's ration was based on pre-war average sales. At first this ration was fixed at a fairly generous

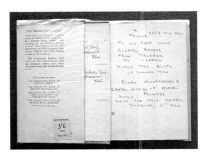

A poignant inscription in a copy of *The Observer's Book of Wild Flowers* from 1941.

60%, but it soon fell to 50% and, for a while, even 30% after supplies of raw materials from Sweden and Finland were cut off. Paper rationing outlasted the war, and not until 1948 did paper again become freely available. Warne could only offer its customers, the bookshops, a quota, and decided to withdraw its travellers since there was no longer any guarantee that orders could be fulfilled. Moreover, some of the younger staff were called up, and on 29 December 1940, the sheet stock in the London warehouse – much of that year's ration – was destroyed in an air raid. In April 1941, William Clowes' warehouse on Duchy Street was also bombed and yet more valuable paper destroyed. However, the Observer's series was classed as educational books and given a partial exemption from rationing. Warne were able to add a small edition of two more nature titles despite the Blitz: *British Freshwater Fishes* (1941) and *British Grasses, Sedges and Rushes* (1942) – as well as keep the earlier books in print. To compile *Freshwater Fishes*, Warne turned to A. Laurence Wells, who had written books for them about aquaria, microscopes and garden ponds. The excellent colour plates were taken, as usual, from the matching Wayside and Woodland volume – which had in

Titles published in 1941-42 during wartime paper rationing.

turn recycled them from a long out-of-print European tome published at the turn of the century. The text of *Grasses, Sedges and Rushes* was based on a book written by Anne Pratt as long ago as 1859, but later published in a revised edition by Warne. As for the pictures, Stokoe had snipped ancient line drawings from *Syme's English Botany* and hand-coloured them himself. There were long delays between printing and publishing at this time, which no doubt reflected local difficulties and staff shortages.

The Observer's Book of Airplanes, also published in 1942, was the first non-nature title. It was the first original book of the series in the sense that, unlike the others, it was not based directly on another book. Nonetheless it was something of a scissors-and-paste job, rushed out to cater for the wartime craze of plane spotting. Its author, a leading light in the Aircraft Recognition Society, was in the aeronautical business and had already compiled a compact aircraft book for Warne, called *Aircraft of Today*. For some reason he chose to write under a pseudonym – 'Joseph Law-rence' were his Christian names. Though the book was revised in 1943 and 1944 to include new aircraft types, only 35,000 copies were printed in total, and the book seems to have been a victim of paper rationing.

Airplanes (1942) was rushed out to cater for wartime aircraft spotters.

27

It is now one of the great rarities of the series. The title 'Airplanes' may have been pitched at the American market, but exports of books were severely limited at this time, and as far as we know it was not sold outside the UK. *Airplanes* was listed as a 'semi-detached' Observer's title – possibly it was seen as a 'one-off'.

There were no more Observer's titles until 1945 when *The Observer's Book of Dogs* by Clifford L.B. Hubbard appeared (it was actually printed in 1944). Like other titles of the later 1940s, it was an austere volume, illustrated only in black-and-white, including the jacket. This was a wholly original work – and hence the first to bear the author's name on the jacket. 'Doggie' Hubbard is well known in the dog world as a journalist and book reviewer. It was a successful title – it was reprinted every year until the 1960s, translated into five European languages, and, like *Airplanes*, helped to broaden the scope of the series. Clifford Hubbard is still contributing book reviews to the Kennel Gazette half a century on, and, proving there is life in the old dog yet, he recently remarried.

Dogs was the only new title to appear between 1942 and 1949. *The House of Warne* describes the immediate post-war years as a particularly difficult and unsettling period.

The years 1945-46 saw the return of the younger members of the staff who had been engaged in various war services, and one of the problems naturally facing the newly formed Board was that of re-absorbing these people back into the business. That this was a problem was in part due to the unsettling influence of the time and the fact also that many of the staff had been away for anything up to five or six years, having gone out as juniors and returned as grown men.....

With [paper] stocks strictly limited, the Company was not too anxious to see its travellers back on the road, taking orders which might have little hope of being executed. Several of these men, feeling rather disheartened in the circumstances, finally accepted jobs with other publishers.....

The golden decade

Though, by 1949, the Observer's series was already 12 years old, 10 of them had been blighted by rationing and other wartime restrictions. It says something about Warne's long-term outlook that they managed to keep it going throughout this time. But, with the end of paper rationing and with its travellers and editorial team back in place after an internal overhaul, the prospects were suddenly much improved. Warne was ready to, in effect, relaunch the series. 'Dick' Billington, known in the firm as 'DB' or 'The Old Man', was appointed managing director in 1946, a post he held until his sudden death in 1960. Billington had been with Warne since 1923, and though 'not a literary man', was thoroughly versed in the mechanics of book production and had his own ideas about what sort of books the company

Two postwar titles which expanded the scope of the series.

should publish. Billington had been involved with the Observer's series from the start, and retained a paternal interest in it, commissioning titles and authors, and expanding the series into non-natural history topics, beginning with *Airplanes* by his friend of pre-war days, Joseph Lawrence Nayler. It was at Billington's insistence that Observer's titles ran up the spine. He thought they looked better that way.

Another key personality of the forthcoming golden decade was A.F. (Albert) Stuart, who became art editor in the late 1940s and remained in that post until his retirement in 1977. Stuart's particular skill was in hand lettering; he had written a book about the subject, and the characteristic fine lettering of Observer's book jackets up until 1960 was his work. He was also responsible for commissioning artwork and photographs for the series, and occasionally contributed drawings himself, as in OB *Geology* and *Flags*. Observer's collectors owe a great debt to him, though his name rarely appears in the books.

Albert Frederick Stuart (1912-1995), designer of the Observer's Books.

From 1949, the old titles were given much-improved jackets, and new titles appeared annually. No longer specifically a nature series, it became more broadly educational, and also remembered that observers look at things like aircraft, buildings and paintings, as well as birds and flowers. Nature subjects did continue to appear – moths, mosses, birds' eggs, fungi – but the new best sellers were the spotter's subjects – like ships, cars ('automobiles'), aircraft and trains ('railway locomotives'). Pets were another popular subject, and *Dogs* was eventually joined by *Horses and Ponies* and *Cats*. Inevitably the variety of new subjects and authors led to widely differing treatments. As *The House of Warne* expressed it, 'Such popular titles as Automobiles and Railway Locomotives have an obvious appeal to the older schoolboy, and they sell in their thousands annually, while the *Observer's Book of Music* by Freda Dinn and the *Observer's Book of Painting and Graphic Art* by William Gaunt cater for the more adult reader'. The appearance of the books also became much more varied, with titles like *Architecture* and *Music* being illustrated by line-drawings, with or without a lithographed over-print. And instead of a picture per page, it became more economic to separate text and plates.

Some new titles were of interest to specific groups of hobbyists rather than the more general appeal of birds and flowers. *Horses and Ponies* was a favourite at gymkhanas, *Ships* and *Locomotives* appealed to model-makers and spotters, *Garden Flowers* and *Cacti* to gardeners, and so on. Many of the ideas for new titles came from outside the firm – as the later sales director, David Traube, recalled, 'they came in by the morning mail, sometimes as suggestions for new titles, occasionally as completed manuscripts'. When I.O. Evans suggested that Warne should 'extend their excellent series of works on Natural History to cover geological subjects', for example, the publisher's response was to suggest that he wrote the book himself. The Observer's Books of *Cacti, Mosses, Pond Life, Lichens, Furniture* were among the many suggestions for titles to come from outside the firm. The extraordinarily successful *The Observer's*

Book of Aircraft was more a matter of chance. The aircraft journalist William Green's involvement in the series began when Warne borrowed some of his photographs of Soviet aircraft for the 1952 edition of OB *Aircraft*. In Mr Green's words,

> I duly supplied the photos, the months passed and I then received galley proofs of the book with a request that I identify the photos that I had supplied. The proofs astounded me. The facts provided were, where accurate, years out of date, but for the most part wildly inaccurate. I returned the proofs, identifying my photos, and commenting that the copy was frightful – not that it was really any business of mine! Frederick Warne responded with a request that I make the necessary corrections for a flat fee – if I remember correctly – of £50. I had no recourse but to rewrite the thing totally, sending it to the publishers and then departing for Canada.

Unable to decide between them, the editor placed both the original and the Green versions in the hands of Gerald Pollinger, secretary of the Aircraft Recognition Society – and, as it happened, a literary agent by profession. Pollinger decided in favour of Green, and promptly drew up a contract in which he proposed Green and himself as joint authors. William Green therefore returned from Canada to find himself co-author of *The Observer's Book of Aircraft*. He transformed it from a simple spotter's guide into a unique annual handbook of the very latest types, or even prototypes, of aircraft. It was at this point that sales began to soar towards 100,000 a year. Gerald Pollinger eventually dropped out in 1960.

It took Frederick Warne a little while to find the right author for the 'jotters and spotters' books of the series.

The 1949 *Aircraft* and its 1952 successor by Green and Pollinger.

Like *Aircraft*, both *Automobiles* and *Railway Locomotives* began in what A.F. Stuart described as 'a general way', before the publishers found Len Manwaring and Henry Casserley, whose knowledge and enthusiasm for their subject made them William Green's terrestrial counterparts. All these books were an austere mixture of facts and figures, photographs and production history – which seems to have been just what their users wanted. The Warne files are full of letters from small boys pointing out some minute error over wheel ratios or jet armament.

The authors of the new titles proved remarkably adept at squeezing a quart into a pint pot. The appeal of the series widened, and titles began to gain respectful reviews. *The Tatler* found *Horses and Ponies* 'the work of a master'. *Architecture* was warmly praised, not least because, in all the best titles in the series, it stuck to the original Observer's ethic of encouraging readers to use their eyes. As the authors, John Penoyre and Michael Ryan expressed it, 'we have written this book for the interested layman who, unwittingly, lives with architecture around him every day.... We hope that he will become aware of it, observe it and understand it for what it is'. To *The Listener*, their book was 'to the intelligent observer, the man who wants to use his eyes to inform his mind, the most useful introduction he could hope to find'. *Ships* was presented 'a true pocket book for "field" use in and around ports, seaside resorts, on holiday cruises – in fact anywhere there is transport by water'. *The House of Warne* selected *Painting and Graphic Art* for particular praise: 'We have always admired Mr Gaunt's book for its conciseness and balanced viewpoint, and both this book and his more recent *Observer's Book of Modern Art* are one-third the price of any similar survey on the same subjects.....'. *The Studio* agreed, calling it 'a miniature gold-mine of information'. The *Times Litt. Supp.* reminded school libraries to order a copy.

Observer's Books from the golden age.

Observer's authors were invariably enthusiasts – though whether amateur or professional depended on their subject. Penoyre and Ryan (*Architecture*) were practising architects, Freda Dinn (*Music*) was a music teacher, and William Gaunt (*Painting*) an art journalist who also painted pictures. On the other hand, Reginald Summerhays, who wrote *Horses and Ponies*, and later the successful *Summerhay's Encyclopaedia for Horsemen*, was a retired solicitor, and Frank Dodman of *Ships* taught art at Bournemouth College. I.O. Evans, who contributed no fewer than three books to the series (*Geology*, *Flags*, *Seashore*), was a civil service librarian and researcher. Since the financial motive was not strong – the going rate at this time was a set fee of about £100 or a royalty of a penny a book – these books must have been products of a passion for education.

In some cases, the authors were their own illustrators, and in design terms these form some of the most satisfactory books in the series with their close harmony of visual and verbal presentation. In the case of *Ships*, artmaster Frank Dobson's drawings, paintings and silhouettes are so lavish that the text seems like a commentary on the pictures. *Architecture* is another well-illustrated title, the full-page drawings being by John Penoyre, while most of the smaller text drawings and the 'visual index' were by his colleague Michael Ryan. Later on, *Lichens*, *Postage Stamps* and *Cathedrals* were similarly author-illustrated, in the latter two cases by the architect author, Anthony New.

The 1950s was perhaps the heyday of the Observer's series, while knowledge was still regarded as wonderful and exciting. Big sales and low interest rates meant that the publishers could continue to illustrate them on a lavish scale, and in colour. Dick Billington worked on the principle that to market a five bob book one had to print so many copies

– and printed they were. Good commercial artists were commissioned for the new natural history titles, like H.D. Swain (*Birds' Eggs*) and Ernest Mansell (*Fungi, Mosses, Pond Life* and *Seashore*). At that time, colour photographs could rarely match artwork in quality. An exception might have been the 'famous Clarke collection of cloud photographs' used to illustrate *The Observer's Book of Weather*, but unfortunately the printing failed to do them justice.

Larger British Moths (1952) by R.L.E. Ford began a new trend among Observer's natural history titles, since here for the first time the text is original, fresh and obviously first-hand, complementing rather than echoing its parent Wayside and Woodland volume (South's two-volume *Moths of the British Isles*). This complementation of titles was taken a stage further in *Pond Life* (1956). Its author, John Clegg, had written a Wayside and Woodland volume on *Freshwater Life*, with an excellent text but rather few colour plates, which meant inevitably that it was more of a classroom book than a field guide. *Pond Life*, on the other hand, presents a wonderful portrait gallery of flora and fauna, from microscopic algae to frogs and newts, and was designed *primarily* as a field guide. The two were a perfect marriage of text and pictures – and for a change, it was the Wayside book that borrowed pictures from its Observer's counterpart.

Larger Moths was the last Observer's book in the integrated layout printed on coated paper, pioneered in OB *Birds*. For the later titles of the fifties and sixties, plates and text were separated. This introduced a new problem, since it meant that the text was continually being interrupted by plates. One solution, used in *Painting and Graphic Art*, *Sea Fishes*, *Lichens* and later editions of *Pond Life*, was to

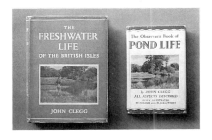

Pond Life (1955) and its Wayside and Woodland companion by the same author, John Clegg.

separate plates from text, but that meant widening the gap between the words and the pictures. Another was to print the plates on the same paper as the text, as in *Bird's Eggs* and *Sea and Seashore*, successfully in the former title though in the latter, the lithographic process used failed to do justice to Mansell's coloured drawings. It was not until the 1970s that improved technology allowed the reuniting of pictures and text, as in the 1977 *Mushrooms* or the 1986 edition of *Pond Life*. Long before then, alas, the problem had been solved in another way – for the economics of modern printing meant that Warne could no longer afford to print three dozen colour plates in a five bob book.

Staying ahead

By the end of the 1950s, the stream of new titles had ebbed to a trickle, and the last few, like *Garden Flowers*, *Cacti*, and *Cats* had less appeal to children than most earlier titles. The series was by degrees changing from an educational one based on spotting to more adult-flavoured pocket reference books. *Cats*, published in 1959, was the last new title for three years. This did not reflect any falling-off of popularity; quite the contrary, the sales were still very healthy indeed and Warne's own lists proclaimed the series to be 'recognised everywhere as an outstanding success and one of the major achievements of British publishing ... used throughout the world in schools and homes'. It seems to have been more a matter of reorganisation, with the sudden death of Dick Billington in 1960, and other internal upheavals. When, in 1962, the next title, *Sea & Seashore*, appeared, lithography had replaced typepress as the printing method, and the colour ration of other new titles was severely cut. In some ways this did not matter much, as the series was running out of nature titles, which depended most on colour. But in the 1960s, costs were increasing and so was the competition. Frederick Warne could not compete with the cheap, mass-produced comics and picture books now dominating the children's literature, and it was now obliged to specialise in 'books for older children .... for those which are instructional and informative....' as the *House of Warne* expressed it. The charming old white jackets of the Observer's Books looked dated; a five-bob book has to stay within mainstream popular taste and this was towards all-colour photographic jackets. Already, *Automobiles* (1959) and *Aircraft* (1960) had been clad in photographic jackets. Most of the other titles followed suit during the sixties, and all of the new titles were in the new style. Only the scalloped margins remained as a kind of Observer's trade mark.

The new titles reflected the growing proportion of titles on architecture (*Churches*), collecting (*Furniture*), fine art (*Modern Art, Sculpture*), transport (*Basic Aircraft, Commercial Vehicles*) and design (*Heraldry, Postage Stamps*). Some complemented earlier titles still in print. The three art books by William Gaunt – *Painting, Modern Art* and *Sculpture* – form a trilogy spanning 2,000 years of world art – they are virtually a 3-volume title. The *Basic Aircraft* books, Military and Civil, too, were designed to complement *The Observer's Book of Aircraft*; it was decided that the former would now catalogue all the main types, while the latter would concentrate on the very latest variants, in a kind of annual fine-tuning. But with new aircraft appearing in bewildering numbers, the subject soon outgrew its Observer's cloths, and in the seventies a new home was found for basic aircraft in the form of double-sized Observer's Directories.

By the mid-sixties, the costs of printing and binding books had reached the point where a five-bob book could barely break even, irrespective of the print-run. The competition was greater now. Sampson Low's 'Dumpy' Books, Collins' Nutshell Series and Longacre's Hippo Books were all catering for the young hobbyist in a similar format and now at a comparable price. There were the very successful 'Teach Yourself' books in their distinctive yellow and black jackets. Hamlyn had also begun to challenge the field in its paperback 'Little Guides' (though, fortunately from our

Postage Stamps (1967), the last new title before the series was redesigned, and its New Observer's Book successor, *Stamp Collecting* (1986).

point of view, they tended to fall apart when the bindings were strained). Blandford was successfully building up a series of all-colour books for naturalists and hobbyists, though at a higher price and in a different style. It must have been a sad day for Warne when, at last, they were obliged to increase the price of an Observer's Book by a shilling, breaking a full 15 years of stable 'five bobbery'. By the time of decimalisation, in 1970, the books were costing 7 shillings or 35p. By this time, the series had stuck at 42 titles – No. 42, *Postage Stamps*, was to be the last new book for nearly five years. By the time the next title appeared, it would be in a new jacket and in a new kind of series.

A Cascade of Titles

The Observer's Book of Cathedrals was published in 1972. Though an old-style colour jacket had been prepared for it, and appeared in advertisements, the actual book had reverted to the gleaming white of the 1950s, with a framed photograph supported by vivid red and black title lettering. The entire series underwent the same facelift, and all future titles were to appear in this format until 1983. They were commonly displayed together by retailers on special stands provided by Warne – rows and rows of glossy white, differentiated only by the title. Such things cost money, and fortunately, in the run-up to decimalisation, Warne had sold a vast number of *Ready Reckoner* (this was before the days of the universal pocket calculator). Part of the profits were used to design and print new jackets for the entire Observer's series in a single operation. Rather than wait for old stock to be sold, Warne's sales representatives made a tour of Britain's bookshops and retailers and rejacketed the older titles on the spot.

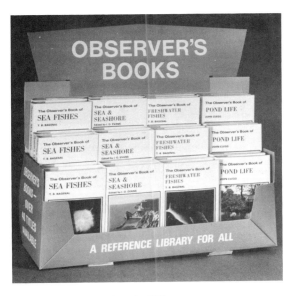

Observer's display carton from the 1970s.

By the 1970s, such books had to reach sales of around 30,000 or even 40,000 copies to enable the publisher to market them at the seventies equivalent of 'five bob' – and that meant that the subjects had to be chosen with care. The scope of the series broadened out to include popular collectables, travelogues and sport. Some titles found ways of incorporating the spotting instinct of sports observers (and material for the colour plates): club shirts in *Football*, ties and badges in *Cricket*, while others resorted to what

Observer's titles from the 1970s in their standard livery.

was to become a regular feature of the later titles, an A to Z glossary of terms, names and places. The aim of the series was now 'to provide an introduction to a wide range of interests', to 'homes, schools and colleges'. As we remember it, few people now collected every title in the series, as they had in the 1950s, and this is to some extent borne out by the print-runs which vary considerably (see our A to Z).

Most titles now had a more specialist appeal. No fewer than five new titles, beginning with *Flowering Trees and Shrubs* and *House Plants,* catered for gardeners, continuing the series begun in the fifties with *Garden Flowers* and *Cacti. Manned Spaceflight* expanded the technical range of the series at the height of the Apollo moon landings, though like the Basic Aircraft books, the *Manned* and *Unmanned*

42

Spaceflight books were eventually given a more commodious home among the Observer's Directories. The year 1973 saw the first travel guide, on *London* (a long-desired title), to be followed by *The Cotswolds*, *Lake District*, *Devon and Cornwall* and *Paris*, all useful little books providing a literary A to Z of villages, museums and beauty spots. Collectors and hobbyists were catered for in a whole roadshow of antiques – *Pottery and Porcelain*, *Coins*, *Awards and Medals*, *Silver*, *Glass*, *Victoriana*, *Firearms* and *Kitchen Antiques*. The original OB *Music* (really classical music) became fairy godmother to titles on *Jazz* and *Big Bands* (originally intended as a single volume, but Mark White's enthusiasm got the better of him), *Folk Song* and *Opera*. There were to be no fewer than three books on the ever-popular pursuit of fishing (plus *Tropical Fish*). There were *Vintage Cars* and *Classic Cars*, as well as annual editions of *Automobiles*. There were even two Observer's Atlases to slip into the pocket. Rather lost in the crowd were the few new natural history titles – on *Seashells*, *Caterpillars*, *Fossils* and *Rocks & Minerals*.

The layout, too, was changing. While *Cathedrals* was similar in style to its predecessor *Churches*, and shared architect Anthony New's excellent drawings, most of the new titles plumped for an integrated format of text and photographs, made possible by new printing machines using offset lithography. Pictures and text were skilfully laid out by A.F. Stuart using scissors and paste – the days of computerised setting was yet to come. Artwork did continue to play an important role in a few titles, perhaps most memorably in the pictorial frieze by the well-known book illustrator, Pauline Baynes, running through *European Costumes* in response to the author's assertion that 'dress is a visual subject'. And the quality and printing of photographs, too, was much higher than in the past. Publishers could by now afford to pick and choose only the very best; those in *London*, *Canals*, *Ancient and Roman Britain* and *Roses* are peaks of excellence. In keeping with Observer's Book tradition, many of the photographs were the work of the authors themselves.

Most titles continued to be little miracles of compression – perhaps more so than ever, since the books were now edited to a rigid 192 pages per title. Different authors espoused subtly different aims. Reginald Turnill hoped to provide an 'interesting and entertaining' introduction to spaceflight in a 'comprehensive reference book in handy form'. *Glass* was written 'for those bitten by the collecting bug'; *Silver* for the 'amateur collector, browser and observer'. Meriel Tilling's *Sewing* was intended as 'a simple reference book for the home'. In *Paris*, Elisabeth de Stroumillo tried 'to convey the variety of ambiences ... as much as to recite facts about its sights'. In *Caterpillars*, David Carter blended the traditional species-by-species approach with a general introduction on biology, parasites and breeding. To extend its appeal to the gardener, garden pests were included as well as more attractive species.

More than most of the earlier books, these were titles to be *read* as well as used. Those by the Geoffrey Palmer and Noel Lloyd partnership are always written with style, and other Observer's regulars like Peter Wheat and Mark White produced a succession of enthusiastic, well-crafted books. A personal favourite is the last title of all, *Opera* by Elisabeth Forbes. A difficult subject to cover, since it is essentially non-pictorial, the author simply described the plots of the world's best-known operas, so that it reads like Grimm's Fairy Tales, a sequence of stories, variously comic, tragic and bizarre. Perhaps the only titles one could happily have

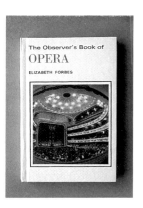

Opera (1982), No. 98 and the last title in the old-style series.

foregone are the two atlases. The coincidence in size between the Observer's Books and Bartholomew's Pocket Atlases must have tempted the Observer's editor, but atlases do not sit well in the series' pocket format. Perhaps the readers thought so too, because the *Observer's World Atlas* is another of the great rarities of the series.

The last years of the Warne Observer's series

By 1982, the firm of Frederick Warne & Co was in financial difficulties. The annual sales of the Observer's books show a dramatic fall from about 1980, even among the best-selling titles. And none of the later titles of the series, had ever sold well. For books of this type, very large print-runs and sales are necessary to bring in any significant profit. Though up to 40,000 copies of each title were printed, many remained unsold. The strategy of diversifying the series had not paid off financially, and what made sense in 1972 looked potentially disastrous ten years later. New titles appeared at a faster rate than ever, but probably none of them were 'earners'. The main problem was competition and increasing sophistication in book production. Collins had revived its Gem Guide series and Hamlyn had also entered the pocket book market. These books made the Observer's look old-fashioned by comparison and only a large investment in printing and promotion could save them. Very likely, the Observer's had lost most of their schoolboy market by 1980, apart from ever reliable titles like *Birds*, *Aircraft* and *Automobiles* (shortly to become *Cars*).

Warne did the only thing it could do in the circumstances. It decided to give the series a major facelift by moving to paperback production, and concentrating on titles that still sold reasonably well. Stocks of OB *Vegetables*, *Kitchen Antiques*, *Opera* etc would remain on sale in their original laminated covers, but would not be reprinted. The paperback Observer's would be given more glamorous-looking 'flexi' wrappers, litho-printed colour pictures and a general freshening up. They were to be called the New Observer's Books.

Other ideas for capitalising on the fame and past success of the Observer's name were explored at this time. Among those considered but ultimately rejected was a lavishly illustrated series of 'King Observer's' in an enlarged A5 format, on subjects like castles, churches and gardens. What Warne plumped for instead was a new series of Observer's Guides on the arts and crafts. This was launched to a fanfare of leaflets, promotions and discount offers, in 1981, but it was by all accounts a financial disaster. The rather drab Guides did not sell – they were far too specialised for this market (see A to Z), and only tarnished the Observer's name. The series was discontinued in 1984.

Had Frederick Warne continued as an independent publishing company, it might have weathered this difficult period of soaring inflation and high production costs. Unfortunately the share value had fallen, and even the sales of Beatrix Potter could not stave off the spectre of looming bankruptcy. We were told that the root of the problem lay in chronic internal inefficiencies in distribution, which ate into the retail profit margin, and also in bad financial advice. As a result, Warne lacked investment funds. Its office lease was about to run out, and one wall was falling down. The Potter copyright was about to expire. But underlying these difficulties was what seems to have been falling morale among Warne shareholders. Most shares in the company were owned by the Stephens family, who had run the company since the 1930s. One senses that 'old-fashioned' family companies like Warne were at a psychological disadvantage in the cut-and-thrust commercial world of the 1980s. Warne had always been a book-led rather than a profits-led company. Its share value had plummeted, though the firm remained a valuable property, with its own warehouse and printing press. In the circumstances, some of the shareholders began to consider selling their shares should an attractive bid be made. One such offer, from Warne's regular printers William Clowes was about to be accepted when it was topped by a considerable margin by a takeover bid from Penguin Books, which proved irresistible. And so, in late 1982, Frederick Warne became a subsidiary of Penguin books Ltd, whose publishing empire also includes Hamish Hamilton, Michael Joseph and Ventura, and which is itself part of the multinational Pearson Group.

The New Observer's Books, already in production before the takeover, would however continue to bear the Warne imprint. The first titles appeared in 1983, and the new style books came complete with their own revolving display stands. Four new titles, which would have brought the original series past the 100 mark, first appeared in this format: Airliners, Warships, Athletics and Tractors, while several older titles were completely rewritten: the old *Postage Stamps*, for example, was now recast as *Stamp*

Collecting while *Commercial Vehicles* became *Trucks*. The New Observer's books were sold at £2.50, compared with £2.95 for the hardbacks still in print, and made a substantially greater profit margin. But, although these books were printed in large numbers, they were not the success that had been hoped for. In all, just 25 titles (in a different numbered sequence) were published in the New Observer's series between 1983 and 1986 (see A to Z for the list). They remain very common secondhand.

In 1987, Penguin Books decided to take the series in hand and re-launch it under the familiar Penguin trademark. Some 26 titles were considered suitable for reissue as paperbacks in newly designed wrappers (see A to Z for list). They were now called Observers (without an apostrophe), with a new logo, a little dot inside the initial O. The remaining stock of Warne hardback Observer's books was withdrawn from sale and either remaindered or pulped. Needless to say it is those titles which are most in demand from collectors today, for their lack of commercial success has made them rare and desirable.

Penguin launched the new 'Observers' with more rotating displays and promotions, and for a few years in the late 1980s they were as prominent in High Street bookshops as were their

A newly designed Penguin Books jacket, reprinted by Bloomsbury Books in the early 1990s.

48

now distant cousins in the 1950s. But there is a limit to the new cloths you can put on an old model. Though the books were still reasonably competitive in price, at £3.50 to £3.95, it gradually became apparent that, however promoted, the series would no longer be sufficiently profitable in the High Street. From 1991, new outlets were found in seconds shops under the Penguin-owned imprint, Bloomsbury Books, and later as Claremont. Oddly enough, these latest manifestations reverted to hardback production and were sold at bargain basement prices, as low as 99p.

By such means, the most successful Observer's titles were kept in print, though we must decide for ourselves whether the dignity of a famous series has been enhanced thereby. No new titles have appeared since the 1980s, and even the annual editions of *Aircraft* and *Cars* now seems to have ended. To most collectors and admirers of the series, it is not their slow decline in recent years we wish to remember as the immortal 'little white books' published between 1937 and 1982. Their place – in publishing history and in our hearts – is secure.

PART TWO

OBSERVER'S AUTHORS

Searching for a quality that unites all the authors of the series, one soon happens on the word *enthusiasm*. The people who wrote these books were enthusiasts who often found ways of *living* their chosen subject, whether as hobbyists or as full-time professionals, or somewhere in the broad grey area in between. Henry Casserley, for example, had a house built to his own specifications so that every room except the bathroom overlooked the nearby railway line. His predecessor on *Railway Locomotives*, Ernest Carter, made a living modelling railway rolling stock. There was no cactus society for S.H. Scott to join, so he started one – and it is now the largest in the world. Many later Observer's authors had a background in education or journalism. Some became journalists during or after a career in sport or the armed services, such as Clarence Jones, a one-time tennis player and coach who represented his country at Wimbledon, or Charles Messenger, a former army officer who recently produced a major television documentary on modern warfare. A smaller but still substantial group are school or college teachers, like Freda Dinn at the Royal College of Music or Harold Priestley, an extramural tutor on local history. Others more or less directly linked with education include Jan Hatley, education officer at Paignton Zoo, or John Clegg and Arthur Jewell, former curators at Haslemere Educational Museum. A minority ran small businesses, or were in the professions, or were members of a scientific institution. One was an actor, another a BBC producer, a third a farmer. What they have in common, though, is the linking thread: their knowledge, their dedication and their passion for their subject.

Many of the earlier authors were of that declining breed, the self-taught amateur enthusiast. Such people are often good communicators because they know what interests others, and have not become bogged down in the *minutiae*. I.O. Evans is a good example, a man with a natural spirit of inquiry, always eager to share his many interests, which included geology, geographical exploration, scientific discovery, Jules Verne, flags and the history of London. Somehow he found time to earn his living as a librarian and researcher at the Office of Works. Grace Pond also worked in an office, but managed to write twenty books about cats, and travel the world as an international cat judge. Reginald Summerhays became one of the best known horse judges of his generation, and was author of a standard work on horses and ponies, yet by profession he was a London solicitor. Richard Ford and E.F. Linssen managed to combine their entomological passions with business by respectively supplying natural history equipment and editing magazines. So did L. Hugh Newman, whose novel occupation was, in his words, a butterfly farmer.

Another linking thread is that Observer's authors (and their publishers too, for that matter) evidently loved books, whether as readers, collectors, writers, or sellers. Clifford Hubbard was all four, apportioning his time between running 'Doggie Hubbard's Bookshop', contributing regularly to *Dog World* and *Kennel Gazette*, and researching canine literature down the ages. Not a few authors turned out a score or more of books during their career. Patrick Moore has probably forgotten how many books he has written or

51

edited, but William Gaunt turned out more than thirty elegantly written books on art, as well as a novel. Some names are virtually synonymous with their subject. Probably no one knows more about medals than Edward Joslin of the firm of Spinks; or about trees than Herbert Edlin of the Forestry Commission, or roses than Michael Gibson, or wild flowers than Francis Rose. In some cases, the series may have awoken new talent. In his foreword, Anthony New modestly revealed that *Postage Stamps* was the first book from his 'inexperienced pen'. Yet it is one of the most original and brilliantly written books in the whole series.

Most authors seem to have written their Observer's book as a labour of love: the financial reward was seldom great. Their real reward was to have popularised their subject as few others have done. Vere Benson's work with the Bird Lover's League or Middle Eastern migrants may be known to only a few, but her memory will be kept green by her association with the best-known bird book of all. And that modest man William J. Stokoe would have been astonished to find his name still in print more than 30 years after his death.

Grouping of authors by profession

Full-time writers, journalists and broadcasters – William Green (aircraft), William Gaunt (painting), Patrick Moore (astronomy), Charles Messenger (military matters), Peter Wheat (fishing), Vivien Batchelor (show jumping), John Woodforde (architecture and collectables), Reginald Lester (weather), Clarence Jones (tennis), Fred Woods (folk music), Reginald Turnill (space flight), Graham Macbeth (motoring), Elizabeth de Castres (silver), Diana Saville (publishing), Elisabeth de Stroumillo (travel), Elizabeth Forbes (music), Gordon Fairley (yachting), Mark White (television producer).

Teachers and other educators – Freda Dinn (Royal College of Music), Frank Dodman (Bournemouth Art college), Geoffrey Palmer (head, London primary school), Harold Priestley (history and head, London grammar school), Robert Croucher (Havering technical college), John Gagg (teacher training and schools advisor), Tina Hearne (RSPCA), Jan Hatley (Herbert Whitley Trust).

Universities, museums and scientific institutions – E.M. Wakefield (Kew), John Clegg and Arthur Jewell (Haslemere Museum), David Carter, Maurice Burton and Frances Atkinson (Natural History Museum), Geoffrey Squire (Victoria & Albert Museum), Kenneth Kershaw, Kenneth Alvin and Francis Rose (London University), Nora MacMillan (Liverpool Museum), Rhona Black (Nottingham University), Allan Jackson and Mary Page (Wye College), Timothy Bagenal (Freshwater Biological Association), W.P.K. Findlay (Forest Products Research Laboratory).

Professions – John Penoyre, Michael Ryan and Antony New (architects), Reginald Summerhays and Lawrence Jones (solicitors).

Businesses – Mary Payton and Nicholas du Quesne-Bird (antiques dealers), Richard Ford (Watkins & Doncaster), Howard Linecar and Edward Joslin (Spinks), Richard Atkinson (company geologist), L. Hugh Newman (butterfly farmer), E.F. Linssen (Leica), 'Joseph Lawrence' (aeronautics).

Civil servants – I.O. Evans (Ministry of Works), H.L. Edlin (Forestry Commission), Brian Davison (Ancient Monuments Inspectorate), 'John Parker' (National Park service).

Others – Lawrence Alderson (farmer), Noel Lloyd (actor).

An A-Z of Observer's Authors and Publishers 1937-1970 (Details of later authors are included on the relevant book jackets.)

Kenneth L. Alvin b. 1927 wrote *The Observer's Book of Lichens* (1963 and 1977). He was a senior lecturer in palaeobotany (fossil plants) at Imperial College, London (1959-1989), now helping the Worcestershire Wildlife Trust. A lifelong enthusiast for lichens, he helped found the British Lichen Society and ran introductory courses on lichen identification for the Field Studies Council. Noted for 'a precise and meticulous manner, and a deadpan, slightly off-beat humour'. He did as much as anyone to promote interest in living lichens, and his Observer's book is still regarded as the best introduction to lichens available. Most of the photographs in the book are his.

Timothy B. Bagenal b. 1925 revised *The Observer's Books of Freshwater Fishes* (1970) and *Sea Fishes* (1972). He is a zoologist and fish expert, graduating at Cambridge and was first a scientist at the Scottish Marine Biological Association at Cumbrae (1949-63) and later the Freshwater Biological Association at Windermere (1963-82), where he was an assistant director. After taking early retirement, he went native in the Lake District, became a sheep farmer and wrote a thesis on lead mining. An expert on brown trout, schelly and other fish, one of his more eccentric papers is titled 'The Fecundity of the Witches of the Clyde Sea Area' (The Witch is, of course, a kind of flatfish). He has also written about the birds and other wild life of remote Scottish islands.

S. Vere Benson (Mrs H.T. Hillier) 1910-1985 compiled *The Observer's Book of Birds* (1937, many times revised). With her sister she founded the Bird-Lovers' League in 1923, to discourage the trade in wild birds and encourage 'Scouts and Guides and young people generally to enjoy and help to preserve birds'. She later wrote several more bird books. Her regular excursions to the Middle East resulted in *Birds of Lebanon and the Jordan Area* (1970), the first specifically devoted to this area and which she illustrated herself. She was a Member of the British Ornithological Union and the first person to record the migration of eagles and other birds along the Lebanon coastline. An acquaintance remembered that 'she left me standing when climbing hills though she was twice my age'. For many years she lived with her sister at Diss, Norfolk and Bow, Devon. She married twice (Hillier, Taylor): Benson was her maiden name.

Richard Billington (called 'D.B.' or 'Dick') d. 1960 represented Warne for 37 years, in the last 14 as Managing Director. Originally with the HMSO, he joined the firm in 1923 as assistant to W.A. Herring of the Production Department. He was made a Company Director in 1940, and Managing Director from 1946-1960, and the responsibility for the Observer's series during that time was primarily his. He had a sound technical knowledge of book production, and was especially interested in illustrated children's books and annuals. He had a flair for 'spotting a winner'. A country lover, a good amateur tenor and a Gilbert and Sullivan addict. In later years known (affectionately) to Warne staff as 'The Old Man' – meaning the boss. His son became manager of Warne's New York house.

Maurice Burton 1898-1992 rewrote *The Observer's Book of Wild Animals* (1971). A zoologist and writer, he spent most of his working career at the Natural History Museum where he was Curator of Sponges 1927-58 and Deputy Keeper of Zoology 1949-58. He is best known for his popular writing and journalism, as a regular contributor to *Illustrated London News* and as the nature notes diarist to the *Daily Telegraph*, which he kept up for 40 years. His 30+ books include the Wayside and Woodland *Wild Animals of the British Isles* (1960) and encyclopaedic works such as *The Story of Animal Life* (1949) and *Purnell's Encyclopaedia of Animal Life* (1970). He kept a menagerie in the grounds of his home, including a dancing crow. His children, Robert and Jane, are also well-known naturalists.

Ernest F. Carter, compiler of *Railway Locomotives of Britain* (1955) was a lifelong railway modelling enthusiast. He was one of the original train-spotters, and by 1932 was designing and marketing model construction kits and building models professionally for Basset-Lowke and others. From 1934-38, he founded and edited The Model Railway Constructor magazine. He wrote at least 20 books and booklets on model railways including *The Model Railway Encyclopaedia* (1950), as well as on physics and industrial chemistry. As a modeller, he was a perfectionist: 'do as the real railways do it and you will not go far wrong'. His brother Kenneth did the watercolour paintings in the original Observer's Book.

H.C. [Henry Cyril] Casserley 1903-1991 edited and revised *The Observer's Book of Railway Locomotives of Britain* (later *British Steam Locomotives*) from 1957 onwards. Over more than half a century he wrote or compiled over 30 books on locomotives and railway

history. Starting in 1919, he also amassed a large personal archive of photographs, an important source of pictures for railway books and magazines. His first book was *Veterans of the Track* (1946) and his last *The Observer's Directory of Steam Locomotives* (1980). A Londoner, he later moved in 1939 to Berkhamsted, choosing a location where he overlooked the mainline railway, and designing his house so that passing trains could be seen from every room (except the bathroom).

John Clegg 1909-1998 wrote *The Observer's Book of Pond Life* (1956) and was natural history adviser to Warne from 1960-1982, commissioning several Observer's titles. For many years he was a museum curator, notably at Haslemere Educational Museum (1949-62), which he transformed from a 'Victorian' institution to a modern educational facility, and later at Torquay Natural History Museum and the Gilbert White Museum in Selborne. He became enthralled by pond life as a boy in his native Ormskirk, Lancs, while catching Great Diving Beetles in a local farm pond. Later ran a small-holding with his wife in Cheshire before becoming RAF photographic officer during the war, and subsequently at the Air Survey Company. He wrote the popular *Freshwater Life of the British Isles* (1952) for Warne, and subsequently other books on freshwater wildlife. In 1958 he helped to establish the Surrey Wildlife Trust. From 1965 he lived in Lake District, studying and photographing pond life as an honorary member of the Freshwater Biological Association and a Fellow (*honoris causa*) of the Linnaean Society.

T.A. [Thomas Alfred] Coward 1867-1933 wrote the book on which *The Observer's Book of Birds* was based. This was the 3-volume *Birds of the British Isles and their Eggs* published by Warne in 1920 and for many years the standard popular handbook on British birds. Coward was a lifelong native of Cheshire, remembered as 'a short thick-set, knickerbockered figure, always topped by a cloth cap'. He spent his first adult years in a firm of bleachers, but from 1900 cut loose on a new course as one of the first full-time naturalists, writing books and newspaper columns, and lecturing, especially on his beloved birds. A great outdoors man, a keen cyclist and a Cheshire character.

Freda Dinn [Winifreda Louisa] 1910-1990, author of *The Observer's Book of Music* (1953), was a lifelong performer and teacher of music. Born in London and educated at Alleyn's School, Dulwich (where Gustav Holst of 'Planets' fame was her tutor), and the Royal College of Music where she was violin scholar. She subsequently taught the violin and viola in the Junior Department of the College and established the Junior Exhibitioner Orchestra, which she conducted herself. After teaching at Trinity College and elsewhere, specialising in early music and recorder playing, she returned to the RCM where became Recorder Professor in 1967 but retired in 1971 because of ill-health. She subsequently built up a large class at a specially built music room at her home in Birchington, Kent, and wrote books on violin, viola and recorder playing techniques. She was firm with her pupils and orchestras, but is remembered with affection as a kind and generous teacher. She never married. Her work at the RCM is recognised by annual Freda Dinn String and Recorder prizes.

Frank E. Dodman wrote and illustrated the *Observer's Book of Ships* (1952, revised many times up to 1990). An art teacher and lecturer by profession, he was educated at Buxton College and Manchester College of Art, and taught at Bournemouth College of Art, becoming head of a department. During the war, he served in the RAF as interpreter of air photographs of shipping and port installations, and lectured Coastal Command aircrews on ship recognition. His lettering, drawing and painting skills were put to good use in *Ships*, one of the most lavishly illustrated books of the series. He was also an authority on ship's figureheads and marine paintings, about which he lectured widely. His publications also include *Merchant Ship Recognition* (for service use), *Ships of the Cunard Line* and handbooks on lettering.

H.E. [Herbert Leeson] Edlin 1916-1976 rewrote *The Observer's Book of Trees* (1975). A forester by profession, he spent his career initially as a rubber planter in Malaya, then in the New Forest raising and planting young trees for the Forestry Commission, and from 1945-76 as the FC's publications officer. He was the most prolific author of his day on tree-related subjects, compiling guides to forest parks and writing a large number of popular works on trees and woodland crafts that have stood the test of time, including the revision of *Wayside and Woodland Trees* (1964). Appointed MBE, 1970. A quiet, somewhat deaf man with a gentle sense of humour, often spotted correcting proofs on railway journeys. He was an active member of all the main Forestry Societies and a regular attender of their outdoor meetings – a friendly, diffident figure who knew his subject inside-out.

I.O. [Iolo Evans] d. 1977 wrote The Observer's Books of *Geology* (1949), *Flags* (1959) and *The Sea and Seashore* (1962). A talkative Welshman and born enthusiast with a flair for journalism, he was the librarian at the Ministry of Works, Lambeth Bridge House, and researched, edited or wrote books and verse in his spare time. He wrote a biography of Jules Verne (1956), attributing his zeal for geology to a youthful reading of *A Journey to the Centre of the Earth*. Childhood visits to the seaside at Swansea Bay and Cornwall encouraged his passion for the sea shore. He was active in the Boy Scout movement, and wrote a number of educational science books for Warne in the 1950s and 60s, such as *Inventors of the World* and *Engineers of the World*. He was elected Fellow of the Royal Geographical Society in 1948, on the proposal of Gordon Campbell, with whom he had worked on a number of books, and Admiral Mountevans (the Teddy Evans of the Scott Expedition).

W.P.K. [Walter Philip Kennedy] Findlay 1904-1985 rewrote *The Observer's Book of Mushrooms* (1977). He was a professional mycologist, specialising in problems of timber decay, based at the Forest Products Research Laboratory, Princes Risborough (1927-58), and later the Brewing Institute Research Foundation, Nutfield. He was also a private consultant, and wrote several books, including *Wayside and Woodland Fungi* (1967) and *Fungi: Folklore, Fiction and Fact* (1982). He was for some years a member of Surrey County Council, and on its planning committee. He was the 1949 president of the British Mycological Society.

R.L.E. [Richard] Ford 1912-1997 wrote *The Observer's Book of Larger Moths* (1952). He was an all-round naturalist, specialising in insects, birds' eggs and geology, and was also much involved in education and nature conservation. He wrote a number of books, including four volumes in Black's Young Naturalist's Series (1950-54) and *Practical Entomology* (1963) in the Wayside and Woodland library, later revised under a new title, *Studying Insects* (1973). From 1940 to 1969, he ran the well-known firm of natural history suppliers, Watkins and Doncaster, initially in The Strand, London, and later in Kent. He is a Fellow of the Royal Entomological Society and the Zoological Society, with long experience of collecting, breeding and reintroducing butterflies, moths and other insects. On retirement he moved to the Isle of Wight to pursue his other love, fossil mammals.

William Gaunt 1900-1980 wrote The Observer's Books of *Painting and Graphic Art* (1958), *Modern Art* (1964) and *Sculpture* (1966). From the 1920s he has been among the most prolific art journalists and critics, specialising in nineteenth century English painting. He contributed regularly to *The Times* and *Evening Standard*, and published no fewer than 32 books on subjects ranging from Turner and Renoir (two favourite painters) to the Surrealists, the Pre-Raphaelites and painters of fantasy. He even wrote a novel, *The*

Lady in the Castle (1956). His Observer's books were much admired for their 'conciseness and balanced viewpoint' and their exceptionally good value. A contemporary at Warnes remembers his 'rugged Spencer Tracey looks' and his charming and gentlemanly manner.

William Green b. 1927 has compiled *The Observer's Book of Aircraft* since 1952, as well as *The Observer's Books of Basic Aircraft Civil* (1967) and *Basic Aircraft Military* (1967). Among many other books about aviation history and current aircraft, he compiled no fewer than six Observer's aircraft directories. Except for a spell in the RAF during and after the war, he has

been a lifelong aviation journalist, starting with *Air Training Corps Gazette* (now *Air Pictorial*). From 1947 he was correspondent to several European and overseas aeronautical journals, and became technical editor, and later editorial director, of *RAF Flying Review* (later *Flying Review International*). On its demise in 1971 he teamed up with Gordon Swanborough to create and launch the monthly *AIR International*, now the largest-circulation European aeronautical journal. He is married with two children.

W.A. Herring d. 1954 was for many years Production Manager and later Director of Warne, and responsible for the earliest Observer's titles. He joined the firm in 1894 and was closely involved in the publication of Beatrix

Potter's writings and artwork. He was appointed a Director in 1940, retired in 1946, but continued his association with Warne right up to his death in 1954. He was an artist and bibliophile, and it is believed that the distinctive style of the early Observer's jackets was his influence, and possibly his own work.

Clifford L.B. Hubbard b. 1913 wrote *The Observer's Book of Dogs* (1945). He is a writer, journalist, editor, bookseller, bibliophile and historian on all dog-related subjects. Since the 1930s, he has written many magazine articles and over 30 books about dogs, including the scholarly *Introduction to the Literature of British Dogs, from 1570* (1949). Since 1972 he has run 'Doggie Hubbard's Bookshop' from his Welsh home. Still attends Crufts dog show regularly, contributes a monthly book column to *Kennel Gazette*, and is researching the literature and historical background to Old Mother Hubbard. He married twice, the second time to a lady less than half his age! 'Canis' (on the early *Dogs* dustwrapper) was a *nom-de-plume* he used in the 1940s.

Arthur L. Jewell b. 1921 wrote *The Observer's Book of Mosses and Liverworts* (1955). Brought up in Battersea, he was a devotee of museums from an early age, and, in 1949, found his niche at Haslemere Educational Museum, 'attracted by Haslemere's community spirit and Fabian leanings'. He began as assistant curator under John Clegg, later succeeding him as curator (1962-88). A natural and local history polymath and keen microscopist, he is a quiet, kindly man with a natural empathy with children. He is remembered at Haslemere by the Arthur Jewell Field Laboratory, and a stuffed bear called Arthur. Awarded Queen's Jubilee Medal, 1977.

Lawrence E. Jones wrote *The Observer's Book of Old English Churches* (1965). A City of London solicitor by profession, he has a passion for churches and their preservation. He was a Diocesan Reader and lectured almost nightly for the benefit of the Historic Churches Preservation Trust. He was also Hon. Secretary of the Friends of Friendless Churches and The Friends of the City Churches. He has written several more books about English churches. He somehow managed to visit interesting churches throughout England without, we are told, being able to drive a car.

Kenneth A. Kershaw was co-author of *The Observer's Book of Lichens* (1963), and drew many of the coloured illustrations. He was a lecturer in botany and later Professor at Imperial College, London, and a colleague of his co-author Kenneth Alvin. He was a pioneer field lichenologist, combining professional specialisation with great field and artistic skills. He is remembered as a lively lecturer, popular with his students. He now lives in Canada, and runs a business dealing in old maps.

Arthur King d. 1964 compiled *The Observer's Book of Garden Flowers* (1957). He spent the whole of his working career with Warne, beginning as a traveller in 1912, becoming Export Manager in the 1920s, and succeeding T.H. Scott as an editor in 1936. His final position in the company until his retirement in 1963 was Town Traveller, going regularly to Paris on company business. His memories helped to fill the earlier chapters of *The House of Warne,* completed by his colleague A.F. Stuart. An educated man, he was a bibliophile and keen gardener.

Joseph Lawrence was the pen-name of Joseph Lawrence Nayler, who compiled *The Observer's Book of Airplanes* (1942) and the 1949 edition of *The Observer's Book of Aircraft.* He was President of the Aircraft Recognition Society, and evidently worked in the aeronautical industry. In the 1930s he had compiled two pocket books for Warne, *Railways of Today* and *Aviation of Today.*

Reginald M. Lester 1897-1976 wrote *The Observer's Book of Weather.* He was a journalist and author with a lifelong interest in weather, writing newspaper columns, magazine articles and popular books. He also produced weather calendars for industrial companies, prepared weather posters for London Underground Railways and visual aid strips on weather for schools. He was made Fellow of the Royal Meteorological Society (1925) and was an active member of the NUJ and the Institute of Journalists, becoming its President 1956-57. He served with distinction in both world wars, in the second achieving the rank of Lt-Colonel.

E.F. Linssen d. 1987 wrote *The Observer's Book of Common Insects and Spiders* (1953). He was of Austrian birth, and retained links with his homeland, including his editor-ship of the journal *Leica Fotografie*. He wrote or edited a number of books on nature subjects, including an anthology of nature quotations, and *Beetles of the British Isles* (1959) in the Wayside and Woodland series, both of which he devoted to the memory of his brother Alex, killed in 1944. His main interests were microscopy and photography, and he combined the two in his magnified studies of insects and other small life. He was also a connoisseur of antiques and the graphic arts. He is remembered as a big affable man and a great enthusiast. He 'travelled extensively in pursuit of his various interests', and on his last journey to the European mainland he apparently disappeared, and his death was announced later. His scientific contributions were recognised in his Fellowship of the Zoological Society and of the Royal Entomological Society.

Charles Stuart MacKinnon wrote *The Observer's Book of Heraldry* (1966). A former RAF pilot and air traffic control officer, he has also been a bookseller based in Tanzania and Oxford, and written books about Scotland's clans and heraldry. His passion for heraldry was inherited from his father, an artist. He is hereditary laird and chief of Dunakin, and owns Dunakin Castle, an ancient ruin on the Isle of Skye. He lived at various times in Africa, Ceylon, India and Malta, and was knighted by the exiled King Peter of Yugoslavia 'for services to the king while in exile'. In the 1970s he retired to France to write novels as a naturalised French citizen. The motto on his coat-of-arms is *L'Audace*.

Ernest C. Mansell 1893-1968 illustrated The Observer's Books of *Common Fungi*, *Mosses and Liverworts*, *Pond Life* and *Sea & Seashore*. He was a commercial artist and art editor on various newspapers and magazines, as well as an illustrator of educational journals and the Children's Encyclopaedia. During the First World War he served in the Royal Flying Corps (later the RAF). For many years he was an art editor to Sir John Hammerton at the Amalgamated Press. From 1947, he became a free-lance illustrator, based at Haslemere. Keen on natural history from childhood, he specialised in nature pictures, one of his last works being *The Complete British Butterflies in Colour*, with L. Hugh Newman. Of his career, he commented that 'sometimes I have been hungry, but unlike many artists I have never starved'.

L. [Len] A. Manwaring compiled The Observer's Books of *Automobiles* from 1957 to 1969 and *Commercial Vehicles* (1966). He lived in Essex, and was apparently a newspaper journalist, notably for *The News Chronicle*. He gave up editing the book after house repairs consumed his spare time.

Patrick Moore b. 1923 wrote *The Observer's Book of Astronomy* (1962). He is perhaps the world's best known astronomer, as the presenter of 'The Sky at Night', the longest-running programme on television, and his 60+ books for star-gazers of all ages. Privately educated, he has been a keen amateur astronomer since boyhood, and is Fellow and sometime President of the British Astronomical Association. He was director of Armagh Planetarium 1965-68. A man of many parts –

bomber navigator during the war, a composer of band music who also plays the xylophone. An endearing personality with his earnest staccato delivery and ill-fitting suits, he has done more to popularise the subject of astronomy than anyone alive. Appointed CBE (1988). Lives in Selsey; likes cricket (supports Sussex), chess, cats, brass bands.

Anthony S.B. [Sherwood Brooks] New b. 1924 wrote and illustrated *The Observer's Books of Postage Stamps* (1967) and *Cathedrals* (1972). An architect and structural engineer, he specialises in conservation and restoration work, especially of churches. Since 1963, a partner in Seely & Paget, and a fellow of Royal  Institute of British Architects. His drawings and beautiful lettering illuminate several books in the series. As for postage stamps, his passion was kindled by a maths teacher 'able to communicate his enthusiasm for both subjects', and he is still an active member of 3 local clubs. He combined his interests by designing several Commonwealth stamps himself. He also wrote three books on cathedrals and abbeys for Constable.

L. Hugh Newman 1909-1993 contributed to *The Observer's Book of Common Insects and Spiders* (1953). He ran a commercial 'butterfly farm' in Kent, inherited from his father, but was more widely known through his journalism, appearances on the radio programme *Nature Parliament*, and later on television. He wrote 20 books about butterflies and other insects, nature gardening and photography. In retirement, he developed a successful photographic agency, now the respected Natural History Photographic Agency. A personable, good-looking family man, who combined a knowledge of the natural world with a sense of style and presentation. His autobiography is *Living with Butterflies* (1967).

Richard T. Parsons edited the first two editions of *The Observer's Book of Automobiles* (1955). In his foreword, Stirling Moss noted that 'all his life Mr Parsons has studied the changing trends of motor car appearances. Now to the accompaniment of facts, figures, photos and history, he has introduced, in this volume, over 80 recognition sketches, thus following the system used so long for ship and aircraft recognition'.

John Penoyre b. 1916 wrote and illustrated *The Observer's Book of Architecture* with Michael Ryan. Educated at St Edwards, Oxford and the Architectural Association's School, in the same year as Michael Ryan. He was a professional architect in private practice from 1939-81, apart from war service. He has also written *Houses in the Landscape* (1978) and *Decorative Plasterwork in the Houses of Somerset* (1994) with his wife, Jane, and contributed architectural drawings to other works. He is presently studying vernacular architecture in his home county, Somerset.

Grace Pond b. 1910 wrote *The Observer's Book of Cats* (1959). She was well-known in the cat world as organiser of the annual National Cat Club show – the largest in the world – for 40 years, and as a globe-trotting international cat judge. She was also on the Council of the Cat Fancy. She wrote or collaborated on some 25 books about cats and often appeared on radio and television. Her love of animals began as a child when her mother gave her a Blue Persian kitten, and she later became a noted breeder of pedigree Blue Persian cats (their portraits are in *Cats* Plates 4 & 7). Much of this was achieved in her spare time, as a secretary and mother of two.

Francis Rose b. 1921 rewrote *The Observer's Book of Ferns* (1965), *Grasses* (1965) and *Wild Flowers* (1978), and was 'editorial consultant' for *Lichens* (1977). He is probably the most experienced field botanist in Britain, equally knowledgeable about wild flowers, trees, grasses, mosses and, most of all, the lichens – of which two species are named *rosei* in his honour. For much of his career he was a university lecturer, latterly as Reader in Biogeography at King's College, London. He is more widely known as a finder, surveyor and conserver of rare British plants. He has written several other books, including the *Flora of Hampshire* and the best-selling *Wild Flower Key* (1981) published by Warne. Lives with his wife at the edge of a Hampshire wood.

Michael Ryan 1916-1974 wrote and illustrated *The Observer's Book of Architecture* (1951) with his colleague, John Penoyre. He was a practising architect, from 1957 an assistant and later senior partner in the firm of Matthews, Ryan & Partners. He was a Roman Catholic, educated at Ampleforth College and the Architectural Association's School of Architecture, and served in the Royal Engineers during the war. 'He was nothing if not controversial, but he was what he was because he valued the qualities of honesty and straightforwardness in all men.' His major work was in industrial and housing sectors, where his practice collected several honours. He was married with four children.

S.H. Scott d. 1967 wrote *The Observer's Book of Cacti* (1958). He was a founder and the first chairman of the successful National Cactus and Succulent Society, and went on to serve it as secretary 1951-1964. He lived in Nottingham and owned a large collection of cacti and other succulents. He was succeeded as secretary by J.W.P. Mullard who revised later editions of the book.

Edward Step 1855-1931 was the real, though posthumous author of many of the early Observer's natural history titles from *Wild Flowers* (1937) to *Ferns* (1950), based on his best-selling Wayside and Woodland books. He was among the most prolific nature writers of his day, completing an average of a book a year from 1881 to his death half a century later, on plants, insects, shore life and nature rambles. He also wrote children's books as 'James Weston'. A self-made man, he started as office boy and became associated with Warne as editor and reader from 1899-1911. His pioneering work as a nature photographer appears in later editions of Observer's *Ferns*, and the paintings of his daughter Mabel in *Trees and Shrubs*. He was a Londoner, remembered as a self-effacing figure with a neat beard, a supporter of Sunday schools and the temperance movement, and 'a pleasant companion in the meeting room and the field'.

Arthur L. Stephens 1874-1955 was connected to the Warne family by marriage, became a Director of Warne in 1919 and was Managing Director from 1928 to 1945. He was interested in educational books, and expanded this part of Warne's list. The decision to launch the Observer's Pocket Series would have been his. He was remembered as 'a quietly dressed and mild-mannered gentleman of the old school', and 'a family man and churchgoer, not without a sense of humour'. His brother, Frederick Warne Stephens and son, Cyril succeeded him.

Cyril Warne Stephens d. 1981. Son of above, he became a Company Director in 1940, Company Secretary in 1945, and Managing Director in 1960-81. He succeeded Frederick Warne Stephens as Company Chairman in 1964. Hence he was involved in the Observer's series at some level for over forty years. Those who knew him recall his old-fashioned courtesy and his tiny 'Dickensian' office in Bedford Street with its box of slightly damaged Observer's books 'there for the taking'. The sometimes unusually narrow page margins of Warne publications has been attributed to Cyril's dyslexia. He was the last of the Warne family of publishers.

Frederick Warne Stephens was uncle of the above and a grandson of Frederick Warne. In later years he was known in the firm as 'Uncle Fred'. He joined the firm in 1903 and became its senior overseas representative, travelling each year to South Africa, Australia and New Zealand on company business. He joined the Board of Directors in 1923 and was Company Chairman 1945-64.

William J. Stokoe c. 1870-1950 compiled and illustrated many of the Warne nature books published between 1925 and 1950, including the first Observer's books. Until 1935 he was Warne's art editor, and his delicate watercolours illustrate several of the books of the period, notably *The Seas* and *The World in the Past* in the Wayside and Woodland series. He retired in 1936, but continued to work for Warne as a compiler of nature books until 1950. He is remembered as a 'precise, rather staid character', said to resemble the bearded King George V. He became a keen naturalist, particularly interested in butterflies and moths, and was, in effect, Warne's natural history adviser from 1936 onwards. As the compiler of six of the first dozen Observer's Books, he is a key figure in the story of the series.

A.F. [Albert Frederick] Stuart 1912-1995 [Known as 'Bert' or 'Stuart'] was art director at Frederick Warne 1949-77, responsible for artwork and picture research. He joined the firm in 1929, and studied art at evening classes, becoming much influenced by Eric Gill. Stuart's own beautiful hand lettering appears on Beatrix Potter, the Observer's series and other Warne jackets, and he also co-authored *Lettering for Brush and Pen* with Quentin Crisp. He was a keen book collector and bibliophile, particularly fond of poetry and the classics.

R.S. [Reginald Sherriff] Summerhays 1881-1976 wrote *The Observer's Book of Horses and Ponies* (1949). A London solicitor by profession, he was a small dapper man, an expert horseman and a well known show judge with experience of 'all classes in Britain, including in hand, under saddle and harness, and various classes abroad'. Mostly in retirement, he wrote 23 books about horses and riding, including Warne's successful *Summerhays Encyclopaedia* *for Horsemen* (1959) which ran into many editions. His last book, written at the age of 88, was *The Donkey Owner's Guide* (1970).

E.M. [Elsie Maud] Wake-field 1886-1972, who wrote *The Observer's Book of Common Fungi* (1954), was one of the best known mycologists (experts on fungi) of her time. The daughter of a Birmingham schoolmaster, she was educated at Swansea and Oxford, gaining a first-class degree in botany and going on to study forest fungi in Germany. In 1910, she was appointed mycologist at  Kew Gardens – one of the first woman scientists – where she remained until her retirement in 1951, rising to Principal Scientific Officer and appointed OBE. She was appreciated for her encyclopaedic knowledge, organisation (and enthusiastic attendance) of fungus forays, and prolific correspondence as secretary of the British Mycological Society. She was joint author, with R.W.G. Dennis, of the popular *Common British Fungi* (1950), illustrated with her own watercolour paintings. She was also a keen photographer. Several fungi are named in her honour. She never married.

A. Laurence Wells compiled *The Observer's Book of Freshwater Fishes* (1941) and *Sea Fishes* (1958) and revised *Grasses, Sedges and Rushes*. From 1937, he wrote or compiled at least six other books published by Warne on garden ponds, aquaria and microscopy. His best known book is *The Microscope Made Easy*, which, helped by its exquisite illustrations, remained in print for 40 years.

John Woodforde 1925-1997 wrote *The Observer's Books of Furniture* (1964) and *Kitchen Antiques* (1982). Educated at Radley College and Jesus College, Cambridge, he became a journalist on the *Evening Standard*, the *Sunday Telegraph*, and the *Daily Telegraph*, on which he was radio critic. He was an accomplished carpenter as well as antique collector, and his literacy output included a number of quirky but successful titles like *The Strange Story of False Teeth*, *The Strange Story of False Hair* (1971) and *The History of Vanity* (1992), as well as books on housebricks, country cottages and farm buildings. He rode a penny-farthing bicycle and played the accordion. An acquaintance describes how he 'cut the figure of a tall, languid, tweedy country gentleman', rambling the byways of scholarship in a perceptive, slightly 'olde-worlde' style.

PART THREE

AN OBSERVER'S A TO Z

Advertisements. The first two Observer's titles, *British Birds* and *British Wild Flowers*, were billed as 'Early Summer Publications from Frederick Warne & Co Ltd' in Warne's twice yearly catalogue of 1937. Its autumn list that year referred to their 'outstanding success', and announced two more titles, *British Butterflies* and *Trees and Shrubs of the British Isles*,

Original trade advertisement for the Observer's series, from Warne's Spring list. of 1937.

both due on sale in January 1938 in the 'same format and style as the first two volumes'. While 'outstanding success' might have been a publisher's 'puff' – though they had sold out, the print-run was modest – they were at least encouraging enough to proceed with the series. The 1938 list presented the first five titles as follows:

> *British Birds.* Compiled by Miss S.V. Benson, giving descriptions of the plumage, size of birds, and information respecting their eggs, nest, food etc.
>
> *British Wild Flowers.* Compiled by W.J. Stokoe, giving descriptions of their leaves, flowers, and other

general characteristics, localities and flowering periods.

British Butterflies. Describing all the British species with an account of the life cycle of a Butterfly, and a descriptive account of the eggs, caterpillar, chrysalis and butterfly of each species, all of which are illustrated in the text.

Trees and Shrubs of the British Isles. Describing the growth, leaves, flowers and fruits of 106 species, with 161 illustrations depicting the leaves and fruits, characteristic boles and full grown specimens of each tree.

British Wild Animals. Describing the life histories of all the British species.

By the end of 1938, the series was being referred to in advertisements as 'the popular pocket "Observer's Books"'. Attention was drawn to their eye-catching colour jackets and strong cloth bindings. The books themselves carried plugs for other Warne publications, and would continue to do so until the 1970s. The earliest ran the complete Wayside and Woodland Series ('a wonderful series of Nature Books') on the rear of the jacket, and Edward Step's 'Come with Me' books (q.v.) on the back flap. Later on, the titles advertised were often chosen for their association with that particular book; for example *Freshwater Fishes* advertised books about aquaria and garden ponds by the same author, while *Garden Flowers* listed a series of gardening books published by Warne, including its parent *The Book of Garden Flowers*. With the expansion of the series, related Observer's Books began to be advertised on the jackets, as opposed to being listed merely on the front flap; for example the back of *Cats* (1959) was used to advertise the Observer's

Books of *Dogs*, *Horses and Ponies*, and *Wild Animals*. Jacket advertisements ceased in 1972, when printed inserts took their place (see Inserts).

In the 1950s, selected titles in the series were advertised in the USA by Warne directly, and in Australia by Warne's trade agents, Methuen, and the Sydney bookseller Angus & Robertson Ltd. It was the broadening of the series into non-nature and world-interest subjects that allowed them to be marketed successfully overseas. None of the specifically 'British' titles were included except *Locomotives*, *Architecture* and *Geology*, for which Warne noted, slightly apologetically, that their subjects might seem to be British 'but their interest is international'.

'Are you Observant?' - America promotes the Observer's Books.

The catch phrase in Australia was: 'Everybody can afford the little books with the big ideas' – though the price there was in fact 8/6, not 'five bob'. Sales must have been reasonably good since Observer's books are common there, and the Australians were eventually to embark on a short-lived Observer's series of their own (q.v.).

The US advertising had a comic book flavour. One leaflet from 1958 shows a man peering incredulously through a magnifying glass at the price of $1.25. 'Are you observant?' it asks. 'Then YOU can't AFFORD to miss THE OBSERVER'S POCKET SERIES. The Reference Book Everybody Can Afford.'

At first, Warne included new Observer's titles along with others in their annual sales leaflet. Soon, however, the

Observer's series was given a leaflet of its own, originally folded to A5 size, later folded again to 'Observer's Pocket size' in the 1960s, and finally given a tall double-Observer size leaflet. In the 1950s, booksellers also received postcards with the new title's jacket on the front and details of the book on the back; from about 1957 these were printed in colour. A child audience was reached in Warne's magazine *Boys & Girls (q.v.)*, which flourished in the 1950s and often carried short features and articles about the Observer's Books and their subjects. Efficient advertising, a network

Display stand from about 1970.

of travellers and the quality of the books themselves made the Observer's books for a while 'the leading source of pocket reference throughout the world'.

In 1972 the Observer's series was revitalised, and a new leaflet stressed their value to the hobbyist as well as the naturalist and outdoor observer. The biggest advertising splash of all came in 1987 when Penguin relaunched the series as 'the ultimate pocket-sized reference books' .... 'whatever the hobby, you'll find it in Observers'. With the books came specially designed cardboard 'counter-packs' and a rotating panel displaying all the titles.

Alcan. A limited number of the 1976 and 1977 edition of OB *Aircrafts* were produced inside a special hard cover for Alcan Booth, a firm of aluminium suppliers to the aircraft industry. There is no dustjacket, but the front board and spine bear an impression of the Alcan logo. Sewn into the front of the book is a 16-page insert full of wonderfully boring details about Alcan. The bindings and text are otherwise of the standard trade edition. Needless to say, these books are rare and sought after by the collector who has everything else.

Special editions of *Aircraft* produced by Alcan Ltd and for the Farnborough air show.

America. Frederick Warne had long been interested in American literature – he used to say that he married on the profits of *Uncle Tom's Cabin* – and he opened a New York office as early as 1881. Subsequent managers there worked hard to promote Warne books in the United States. The most successful Observer's titles were *Automobiles* and *Aircraft*, and one not uncommonly finds copies with a dollar price printed at the top of the inside flap of the dustwrapper and the sterling price at the bottom. It was a policy of thrift – in this country the dollar price was clipped, in the States, the sterling price. Some 44 Observer's titles carry a Library of Congress Catalogue Card Number. Not surprisingly, these tend to be the more internationally orientated titles of the series, though they include every title between No. 29 (*Flags*) and 66 (*Farm Animals*), and apparently none after that. In the 1970s, some 20-30 Observer's titles were listed in the catalogue of Scribners of New York, and in the 1980s Warne briefly had a sales arrangement with Arco Books. Actual sales in America are unknown to us: evidently Warne did not keep separate accounts.

Apostrophe. The apostrophe in the series title 'Observer's' establishes a certain intimacy – the Observer in question is not only an individual but is none other than the person using the book. The apostrophe remained in place throughout the life of the mainstream series. But when Penguin relaunched the books in 1987, it was omitted. The change signified that 'Observers' was now a brand-name – and an ungrammatical one at that. The 'Observer' was no longer a person but a book. Advertisements now referred to the 50th anniversary of 'the first Observer' ..... 'join us in celebrating 50 Observers years'. Presumably one joined in by buying the book.

One former Warne editor told us he was once summoned

by the Observer newspaper and threatened with legal action for use of the Observer name. The paper changed its tune when it learned that the Observer's series had been running for half a century!

Atlas. Since the nineteenth century, Warne had acted as trade agents for the well-known firm of Scottish cartographers, John Bartholomew & Son. Bartholomew's Atlases used a distinctive colour layering of contours, invented by the original John Bartholomew himself. By coincidence, the pocket atlases produced by Bartholomew since the 1880s were similar in size to the Observer's Books. In 1976 Warne persuaded Bartholomew to allow them to publish the long-running *Tourist Atlas of Britain and Ireland* as a title in the Observer's series. The text pages were printed by Bartholomew, and only the bindings were in the familiar Observer's livery. It was followed in 1981 by an Observer's version of that other hardy perennial, the

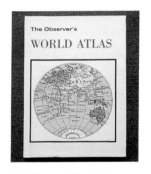

The Observer's World Atlas, broader than the other titles to accompany the Bartholomew's maps.

World Pocket Atlas, in print since 1886. The pages of *World Atlas* are a full centimetre wider than the other books in the series, so that the spine pokes out when arranged on the shelf with its companions. Today it is one of the rarest and most sought-after Observer's Books, although it was a series mismatch in more senses than one.

Australia. In 1979-81 a series of eight down-under titles were published by Methuen of Australia by agreement with Warne (see colour plates).   Though obviously intended primarily for the home market (and New Zealand), Warne took about 500 copies of each title for sale in the UK, mainly for libraries; they retailed in the UK at £1.95, but only a few large bookshops stocked them. The Australian Series had a similar format and layout to the British one, with laminated boards and with the title picked out in red letters. They bore the familiar Observer's logo on the spine, while the series number was prefixed by a capital A (see below). *Birds of Australia* was also available in paper covers, trimmed square with the pages, and with miserable glued-in pages that soon crack and fall out. None of the Australian titles was reprinted and today they are quite scarce, not only in Britain but also, it seems, in Australia too. Around £25 is the going rate now, though dealers will often hold out for more.

The bowl-shaped hill on the *National Parks* cover was amusingly doctored with a sprig of holly by an Observer's enthusiast and sent to friends in Christmas 1993 as the exciting new discovery 'Xmas Puddings of Australia'.

List of titles

A1. *The Observer's Book of Snakes and Lizards of Australia* (1979). By David McPhee. 176 pp. ISBN 0-7232-1650-9.

A2. *The Observer's Book of Birds of Australia* (1979). By Pat & Peter Slater. 224 pp. ISBN 0-7232-1651-7.

A3. *The Observer's Book of Steam Locomotives of Australia* (1979). By David Burke. 260 pp. ISBN 0-7232-1652-5.

A4. *The Observer's Book of Civil Aircraft of Australia and New Zealand* (1979). By Timothy and Elizabeth Hall. 224 pp. ISBN 0-7232-1653-3.

A5. *The Observer's Book of Sailing Craft of Australia and New Zealand* (1979). By Peter Campbell. 270 pp. ISBN 0-7232-1654-1.

A6. *The Observer's Book of Rocks and Minerals of Australia* (1979). By Oliver Chalmers. 256 pp. ISBN 0-7232-1655-X.

A7. *The Observer's Book of National Parks of Australia* (1981). By Alan Fairley. 176 pp. ISBN 0-454-00199-1.

A8. *The Observer's Book of Wildflowers of Australia* (1981). By Alan Fairley. 128 pp. ISBN 0-454-00242-4.

Automobiles. This title was originally listed (in the Warne catalogue of January 1955) as The Observer's Book of Motor Cars. Automobiles was substituted at the last minute, partly with sales to the USA in mind, but also because the industry was then known worldwide as Automobile or Automotive. A special version of OB *Automobiles* (1955) was sold in USA, priced only in dollars and with American cars substituted for British or foreign ones. But the book shared the same printer's code and edition as the home version. Automobiles finally became 'Cars' in 1987.

Binders' marks. On certain Observer's Books printed between 1953 and 1977 you find letters or a strange squiggle stamped on the back of the rear board. These are binders' marks, and they indicate that the books were bound by someone other than the printer. It was normal practice for Warne's regular printers to bind and case the pages themselves. However there were times, especially among the slower selling titles, when unbound sheets would be stored in Warne's warehouse, and bound as required. At one time, the printers would store sheets free of charge, and more or less indefinitely, but from the 1960s many began to charge for storage. As a result, more stock was thereafter held by Warne for contract binding.

Five different binder's marks have been found. The commonest is 'N' or 'n'. This indicates the Newdigate Press, a binding company owned by Warne. It is probable that a 'squiggle', which could be interpreted as a curly 'n', means Newdigate too, since it tends to be found on the same titles.

Binder's marks on the book boards are confined to certain printings.

OB *Lichens*, for example, has been stamped at different times with 'N', 'n' or 'curly n', suggesting a common binding source. *Geology*, which uniquely among Observer's Books was printed 'in-house' by the Warne-owned Eden Press, is another of those which regularly carry a stamped 'N' or 'curly n', suggesting that it too was bound in-house by Newdigate. The 'D' is probably Dorstel, a London-based firm of binders, who occasionally took on work for Warne. 'K' is likely to be the now defunct Kemp Hall of Oxford.

N	1954-56, 1963-77	Titles: *Geology* (1954-56), *Aircraft* (1955-56), *Fungi* (1954), *Garden Flowers* (1969),*Cats* (1963-77), *Sea & Seashore* (1965-75), *Lichens* (1966).

n	1966	*Lichens* (1966).
K	1953-57	*Aircraft* (1954-56), *Birds' Eggs* (1954-67), *Flags* (1959-66).
D	1969-75	*Birds' Eggs* (1969-75), *Flags* (1971).
'curly n'	1956-66	*Trees* (1960), *Geology* (1957-62), *Aircraft* (1957), *Insects* (1964), *Birds' Eggs* (1958), *Automobiles* (1956), *Garden Flowers* (1965-66), *Cats* (1963), *Sea & Seashore* (1962-65), *Lichens* (1963-66).

Bindings.   Until about 1955, Observer's Books were bound in linen cloth.   For a few years in the late fifties this was replaced by an artificial material called 'Milskin', which is embossed to give the appearance of cloth.   Later still that was replaced in turn by a synthetic mock-leather material, widely used in the publishing business, called 'Fabroleen'. From 1980 the books were bound in laminated boards, with a surface point-embossing which varies in intensity from book to book, while the 1985 editions of *Butterflies*, *Birds* and *Trees* are completely smooth.   In the first few years of the series, the boards were secured with ribbon ties, which show beneath the endpapers.

The board wrappers come in a variety of colours – we have traced at least 17, not counting shades.   They seem to have been chosen more or less randomly and without much attempt to match colour and title.   The most popular colour was red, used for 11 titles, followed by tan (10), green (10), blue (8), cream (7), dark blue (6) and light grey (6).   The least popular choice was black, used for *Big Bands* only. The colour often changed during the lifetime of a title:

Bindings from
different periods
1937-80.

Geology, for example, began life as dark green (1949-52),
then changed to various tones of tan, cream or (appro-
priately enough) 'stone' (1953-74), and finished up as brown
(1974-79). *Moths* started as blue, before switching to dark
blue, tan and finally cream.

The quester for rarities will find plenty of examples of
'wrong' colours. At least twelve examples are known: for
example, the 730.153 printing of *Moths* was issued in red
bindings with black letters, while part of the 804.962
printing of *Wild Flowers* is in lurid orange with gilt letters.
This is territory for the true specialist; these variations no
doubt resulted from temporary shortages of binding
material; they are of no particular significance, but this is
precisely the sort of thing that would have a philatelist
jumping for joy.

There are a few more oddities. The cased bindings of
Vintage Cars and *Classic Cars* were slightly too large for

the contents, so that the boards converge slightly. They are also slightly taller than the other titles. *World Atlas* is even more of a misfit, being several millimetres broader than its fellows.

Boys & Girls. Throughout the 1950s and well into the 1960s, Warne published a monthly 8-page news-sheet for children containing 'news of your favourite books and authors'. Needless to say the 'favourite books' were those published by Frederick Warne. Among the topics were short articles on Observer's Books, consisting of short extracts from the books, and a few introductory paragraphs based on the jacket blurb. While *Boys & Girls* was really a form of advertising, it also reflected Warne's interest in education. The news-sheet was 'available free to all children, parents, teachers and librarians'. Each issue contained 'authentic articles of topical interest, serial and short stories', 'at least two pages of Nature Study' and a Pen-friends' section, as well as occasional short poems. The main recipients seem to have been junior and secondary schools where, according to the editors, 'it is most popular'.

'British'. From *British Birds* (1937) to *British Birds' Eggs* (1954), all the Observer's natural history titles plus *Architecture* contained 'British' in their title. This was perfectly accurate – the subject matter of these books was indeed confined to the British Isles (none of the 'and Northern Europe' nonsense then), whereas that of *Aircraft*, *Music*, *Dogs*, *Horses* and (to a smaller extent) *Ships* was international. We should recall that in the formative years of the Observer's series, Britain was still the motherland of a worldwide trading empire, and that one of the most successful publishing ventures of the 1940s had been a series of books called Britain in Pictures. Foreigners were expected to take an intelligent interest in what Britain had to offer.

'British Birds' Eggs' – a short-lived jacket.

When, in 1954, Warne decided to drop the word 'British' from all Observer's titles, it was ostensibly to boost sales in Eire. Ireland was by then being travelled regularly by Warne salesmen, who soon found that 'British' was a barrier to success. It was from about this time that the term 'of Great Britain and Ireland' became the usual currency of book publishers. Perhaps, by this time, the Observer's Books were so well known that the word had in any case become redundant.

'British' or 'in Britain' returned to *Steam Locomotives* (1974), *Awards and Medals* (1974), *Sea Shells* (1977), *Folk Song* (1980) and the second edition of *Coins* (1980), to show that the subject matter was specifically British.

Claremont. An imprint of Penguin Books which reprinted 12 Observers titles in hardback in 1996. The hardback titles, which could be obtained directly from Penguin's cash sales service at £1.99 each, are as follows: *Birds, Canals, Cats, Dogs, Horses and Ponies, Insects, Pets, Pond Life, Trees, Wild Flowers, Rocks and Minerals* and *Tropical Fishes.* By the time this book is printed there may be more. Or there may be none. The book trade is like that.

Collecting. What is a complete collection of Observer's books? At its most straightforward level, it could be the 97 numbered books of the mainstream series (plus this one).

But if the collection included every jacket variation, it would amount to 368 books. If you went mad and included every printing, you would need something like 750 books. Add a full set of New Observer's, Observer's Directories, Australian Observer's, Cyanamids, etc, etc, and a full collection would not be far short of 1,000 books. At least a couple of such collections do exist, and every title, jacket and printing has been meticulously catalogued. Most of us would be satisfied with a basic collection. A popular aim is a complete run of first editions in contemporary jackets. In the past these could be built up relatively cheaply, if slowly. Today, while more secondhand booksellers stock the series, the prices of the scarcer books have risen to match the demand, though there is still a good chance of finding serendipitous bargains in unexpected places. Runs of the annually printed titles, *Aircraft* and *Automobiles*, are also a popular target, and the same people often collect editions of *Ships*, *Railway Locomotives* and the Observer's Directories. A feature of collecting is that once one's aim has been achieved, the feeling is less one of satisfaction than of deflation. For this reason, the once little regarded lanes and cul-de-sacs of 'Observerology' are now full of activity – Down-Under titles, Cyanamids, Puzzle Books, Picture Cards *et. al*.

Condition is entirely a matter of personal choice. A jacket is regarded by most collectors as essential. Collectable books are graded from 'Reading Copy' (downright unhygienic) to Fair (Battered), to Good (i.e. Not Very Good), Very Good (Passable), Fine (Good) and Mint (Very good). For the earlier books, you may have to make do with Very Good or even Good copies. Observer's books generally received heavy usage. Early printings of the more pocketable titles like *Birds*, *Wild Flowers*, and *Horses and Ponies* nearly always look tired and grubby. The periodic replacement of poor copies with better ones accounts for the large number of 'swops' around in Observer's collector's circles, establishing a kind of cascade – one man's discard is another's find. Even the more recent titles of this series are often in poor condition, not so much through wear-and-tear as sunning, during which the title fades away while the rest of the book turns brown in sympathy.

Cyanamids. In 1980, a firm of agricultural products, Cyanamid Ltd, obtained permission to print special dust-jackets for thirteen Observer's titles for use as an advertising gimmick. Printed between 1980 and 1982, they are known by collectors as 'Cyanamids' (see colour plates). A compliments card accompanying each book suggests that they were given away to customers. Twelve of the jackets advertise a product called 'Avenge', a selective poison used to control wild oats. The thirteenth and last jacket, *Heraldry*, advertised 'Stomp', a general purpose weed-killer. The books were issued in series of four, each with a distinctive jacket design. The first four are the plainest, with the 'Avenge' motif emblazoned in red in one corner. The 1981 series are more attractive, and their stylish designs reflect the contents of the book. The third quartet all bear a number "6" design,

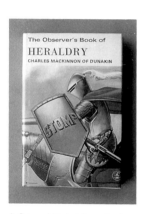

A Cyanamid jacket from about 1982.

apparently because Insects have 6 legs and some Firearms are known as 6-guns. The odd-man-out is *Heraldry* which shows an armoured knight with 'Stomp' on his shield. The designer is unknown.

On the back of eight of the jackets is a blurb thought appropriate for the title. *Birds*, for example, finds common ground between owls and weed-killers:

'The Short-eared owl (page 117) hunts two ways – by day and by night, just as AVENGE plays the dual role of killing wild oats and controlling early mildew.....'

A stellar observation is made on the *Astronomy* jacket.

'Sirius is the brightest star visible from Britain, standing out from all others in the sky (pages 31-35), as AVENGE is the most outstanding wild oat herbicide.'

The stylish Cyanamid jackets are in great demand among keen collectors, who may be willing to part with upwards of £25 for a mint copy. The exact number printed is not known. According to a former sales representative of Cyanamid GB, the books were posted to customers over a period of three years at the rate of one each month for the first four months in 1980, 1981 and 1982, and the last one *Heraldry* was sent in November 1982. The firm has been unable to assist further with our enquiries.

Below are the details of each title given a Cyanamid jacket, together with their print number – the last three figures give the month and year of printing.

| JACKET 1 | 1/1980 | on No. 1 | BIRDS | 559.1177 |
| JACKET 2 | 2/1980 | on No. 4 | TREES | P5828.379 |

JACKET 3	3/1980	on No. 5	WILD ANIMALS	1785.178
JACKET 4	4/1980	on No. 32	ASTRONOMY	2656.877
JACKET 5	1/1981	on No. 22	WEATHER	1447.580
JACKET 6	2/1981	on No. 34	MODERN ART	D6365.1080
JACKET 7	3/1981	on No. 55	AWARDS & MEDALS	8.774
JACKET 8	4/1981	on No. 69	COINS	No code
JACKET 9	1/1982	on No. 17	INSECTS	2725.478
JACKET 10	2/1982	on No. 49	CRICKET	0094.1279
JACKET 11	3/1982	on No. 75	FIREARMS	2701.282
JACKET 12	4/1982	on No. 63	TOURING ATLAS	1554.282
JACKET 13	11/1982	on No. 41	HERALDRY	D6113.1279

Directories. Between 1961 and 1984, Warne published 14 books covering aircraft, ships, vehicles and spacecraft in greater detail than was possible in their Pocket Series counterparts. The first ten were published in an unusual horizontal format, exactly twice the size of an Observer's book. The last four were larger still – nearly quadruple-sized. Stressing their allegiance to the parent series, Warne called these books the Observer's Directories. They were reference books for the serious enthusiast, in a suitably spacious format. The first title, *The Observer's World Aircraft Directory* (1961) was a spin-off from the ever-popular *Observer's Book of Aircraft*, and by the same author, the industrious William Green. But for many years, this spin-off was also a one-off and it was not until 1969 that *World Aircraft* began to multiply into ever more specialised aircraft books, joined by Directories on railway locomotives, spacecraft and military vehicles. Reginald Turnill's *Spaceflight Directory* (1978) showed how far spaceflight had progressed since his earlier books in the Observer's Pocket Series, so much so that a directory-sized volume was now needed. This was also true for the two

Basic Aircraft titles, which soon went out of print in the main series, but resurfaced as Observer's Directories in 1974, in which format they were more successful.

The four Directories on military vehicles by Bart Vanderveen of the Dutch Olyslager Organisation, are designed to deal with separate periods, though this is

An Observer's Directory from the 1970s.

not always plain from the title. The first, *Fighting Vehicles Directory* (1969) apparently broke new ground as the first reference book to deal with the neglected *unarmed* motorised vehicles used in the Second World War. *Military Vehicles* which followed dealt with postwar motor vehicles. The later *Army Vehicles*, on the other hand, deals with motorised vehicles used by the world's armies *before* the Second World War. The last of the quartet, *Modern Military Vehicles*, concentrates on the very latest types. There was a special market for such books among war-gamers and military modellers, both in Britain and in English-speaking countries overseas.

The last title, *US Naval Developments* (1984) was listed by Warne as an Observer's Directory, and is regarded as such by collectors, though it does not match the rest of the series. The book is not really from the Warne stable at all. It was first published in the USA by Nautical and Aviation Publishing Co., and the Warne book differs from it only in the jacket. This book seems to have been designed to accompany *Warships*, also published in 1984 in the New Observer's series.

The first two titles published in 1937.

The first all-colour Observer's jackets, introduced in 1938.

A full run of *The Observer's Book of Automobiles* from 1955 to 1963.

This complete run of *The Observer's Book of Railway Locomotives* (later *British Steam Locomotives*) illustrates the changing design of the series from 1955 to 1990.

Some examples of scarce and sought-after Observer's jacket variations. Most of these jackets had a short shelf-span and are confined to a single printing.

A complete run of the short-lived Australian series of Observer's Books.

The Observer's Book of
CIVIL AIRCRAFT
OF AUSTRALIA AND NEW ZEALAND
TIMOTHY & ELIZABETH HALL

The Observer's Book of
STEAM LOCOMOTIVES
OF AUSTRALIA
DAVID BURKE

The Observer's Book of
BIRDS
OF AUSTRALIA
PAT & PETER SLATER

The Observer's Book of
SNAKES AND LIZARDS
OF AUSTRALIA
DAVID McPHEE

The Observer's Book of
WILDFLOWERS
OF AUSTRALIA
ALAN FAIRLEY

The Observer's Book of
NATIONAL PARKS
OF AUSTRALIA
ALAN FAIRLEY

The Observer's Book of
ROCKS AND MINERALS
OF AUSTRALIA
OLIVER CHAMBERS

The Observer's Book of
SAILING CRAFT
OF AUSTRALIA AND NEW ZEALAND
PETER CAMPBELL

Examples of the New Observer's Books and the Penguin Observers series, published in the 1980s.

These special jackets advertise brands of agricultural chemicals. They were apparently issued free to customers during the early 1980s, and have since become collectables.

The Observer's Book of
TREES
HERBERT L. EDLIN

The Observer's Book of the
INSECTS OF THE
BRITISH ISLES
E. F. LINSSEN

The Observer's Book of
COINS
HOWARD LINECAR

The Observer's Book of
AWARDS & MEDALS
EDWARD C. JOSLIN

The Observer's Book of
MODERN ART
WILLIAM GAUNT

The Observer's Book of
HERALDRY
CHARLES MACKINNON OF DUNAKIN

The Observer's Book of
CRICKET
PETER SMITH

The Observer's Book of
ASTRONOMY
PATRICK MOORE

Examples of foreign printed translations of Observer's titles.

The black-and-white jackets of *Ferns*, *Lichens* and *Common Fungi*,
destined for a short life in the early 1970s.

Today all these books are out-of-print and are becoming scarce secondhand, though one still comes across them in reference libraries. Very likely the unusual horizontal format led to strained bindings and a greater wastage than usual, especially as they also sat awkwardly on most library shelves. Moreover such technical books become outdated quickly unless revised regularly, and hence are thrown away. The most likely places to find them are bookshops specialising in militaria, and book sales held by aircraft-spotting, model-making and war-gaming societies. Most sell for something around the £10 mark.

D1. *The Observer's WORLD AIRCRAFT Directory* (1961). By William Green. Price 15/-. 354 pp. Print no. 512.561. Originally issued in a matt dust-jacket, but later laminated.

D2. *The Observer's FIGHTING VEHICLES Directory* (1969, revised and enlarged in a new jacket 1972). By Bart H. Vanderveen. 25/-, later £2. 340 pp. Print nos 932.469; 1058.572.

D3. *The Observer's MILITARY VEHICLES Directory* (1972). By Bart H. Vanderveen. 325 pp. £2.50. 1999.272.

D4. *The Observer's BASIC MILITARY AIRCRAFT Directory* (1974, reprinted 1975). By William Green and Gordon Swanborough. 224 pp. 508.573; 170.175. Both hardback and limpback versions were sold.

D55. *The Observer's BASIC CIVIL AIRCRAFT Directory* (1974, reprinted 1975). By William Green and Gordon Swanborough. £2.95. 224 pp. 813.374; 171.175.

D6. *The Observer's ARMY VEHICLES Directory* (1974). By Bart H. Vanderveen. £4.95. 378 pp. 814.474.

D7. *The Observer's SOVIET AIRCRAFT Directory* (1975). By William Green and Gordon Swanborough. £3.25. 256 pp. 51.874.

D8. *The Observer's AIRLINES AND AIRLINERS Directory* (1975, revised in new dustjacket 1980). By William Green and Gordon Swanborough. 384 pp. £4.95, 189.375. £9.95, 1304.979.

D9. *The Observer's SPACEFLIGHT Directory* (1978). By Reginald Turnill. 384 pp. 2638.977.

D10. *The Observer's Directory of BRITISH STEAM LOCOMOTIVES* (1980, reprinted 1981, 1982). By H.C. Casserley. 240 pp. 0.7232.2413.7.

D11. *Observer's Directory of MILITARY AIRCRAFT* (1982). By William Green and Gordon Swanborough. Revised and enlarged version of D3. £9.95. 256 pp. 0.7232.2796.9.

D12. *Observer's Directory of ROYAL NAVAL SUBMARINES 1901-1982* (1982). By M.P. Cocker. £9.95. 128 pp. 0.7232.2964.2.

D13. *World Directory of MODERN MILITARY VEHICLES* (1983). By Bart H. Vanderveen. £14.95. 256 pp. 0.7232.3165.6.

D14. *U.S. NAVAL DEVELOPMENTS* (1984). By Jan S. Breemer. £14.95. 194 pp. 0.7232.3234.2.

Dogs. A term of abuse, used by booksellers to describe books that no one buys. In the 1970s a number of Observer's Books fell into that category, but we will not name them. It has nothing to do with *The Observer's Book of Dogs*, which has had retailers wagging their tails for more than half a century.

Dustjackets. One of the things that establish a uniform series of books is trademark packaging – that is, the books' dustjackets. Whichever genius decided to issue the Observer's Pocket Series in the now familiar white jackets knew what he was doing. It not only helped to make Observer's Books instantly recognisable – a useful asset to retailers scanning the catalogues – but also signalled their status as serious pocket reference books, for in the book trade white is the colour of seriousness. From the beginning Observer's jackets were intended to be an important part of the book, and were designed with care, not only for their aesthetic quality (though partly for that) but for their sales potential. Given their low price and even lower unit profit margin, it seems amazing they were given jackets at all.

Until 1960, most of the Observer's jacket designs were decorated and lettered individually by a graphic artist. From the late 1940s, this became the task of A.F. Stuart, an admirer of the beautiful lettering of Eric Gill, whose clear, elegant style is evident in Stuart's own work. Stuart would copy meticulously the ornate lettering of the first Observer's jackets, and most of the attractive jackets of the 1950s are lettered by him. On some titles he cut the letters to suit the subject, so that, while the wildlife titles adhered to the original ornate style of lettering, *Airplanes* was given hollow block letters (like a tubular airframe?), *Music* 'arty' lettering, *Architecture* Roman lettering inspired by Eric Gill, *Weather* leaning 'windblown' letters, and *Geology* elaborate triple-lined letters, like veins running through marble. The first jackets of *Dogs* and *Horses & Ponies* were given 2-colour letters, perhaps to brighten them up. Stuart remembers as the trickiest job of all those terrible wavy lines on the upper and lower edges of each jacket. So well did he succeed that perhaps few have realised that these lines were not at first mechanically produced but drawn freehand. When title lettering began to be reproduced from type, in the 1960s, the jackets lost much of their charm and individuality.

The first two jackets of the series were also the dullest (though no duller than most book wrappers at the time). When they first appeared in 1937, *British Birds* and *British Wild Flowers* were given buff-coloured jackets on stiff paper similar to the contemporary Wayside and Woodland titles, and bearing modest blue ink drawings of their subjects. But the series style was already set in the characteristic ornate title lettering, the scalloped edges and the wavy lines, echoed in the drawings by water in the case of the kingfisher, and heaven knows what in the case of the bluebells – perhaps they were meant to be cut flowers in a vase. Another feature then favoured by Warne was the up-front delivery of 'key points': '200 illustrations in colour and black and white', read the jacket blurb for *British Birds*. '226 species described'.

The original jackets must have been deemed inadequate, for within a few months they were replaced by more brightly

The Mother Nature books, original home of the early Observer's jacket pictures.

This plate from a Mother Nature book published in 1931 was borrowed seven years later for the jacket of *The Observer's Book of Birds*.

coloured ones printed on white surfaced paper. However, the illustrations chosen were far from sophisticated. For some reason, they were taken not from the books themselves but from children's books published by Warne in previous years. The original perch of the mistle thrush on the *Birds* jacket was on a plate entitled 'Some Feathered Favourites' in *Warne's Book of the Country*, first published in 1935. The rather impressionistic foliage on *Trees and Shrubs* came from a plate entitled 'In the Bluebell Wood' in the same book. The others are clipped from Warne's 'Mother Nature' series by Jane Lucas, first published in 1931 and still on sale in the 1950s. Her picture on *Wild Flowers* is borrowed from Plate 1 'Buttercup Flowers and Fruits' in *Mother Nature's Garden*; the cabbage whites on *Butterflies* from Plate 1 in *Mother Nature's Babies*; and the water voles on *Wild Animals* have paddled out of Plate 2 in *Mother Nature's Water Creatures*. By today's standards they seem astonishly crude, torn from their context and casually trimmed to fit so that, in the case of *Wild Animals,* the reflection of a moorhen floats along without the parent bird, while one of her chicks has been cruelly severed from its four siblings. Only the rather charming buttercups from

Wild Flowers would gain a pass grade at GCSE art. One can only assume that the brightness of the jacket was deemed more important than the quality of the illustration, or that the books were then intended for children.

From *Freshwater Fishes* (1941) onwards, the jacket illustration was generally taken from the body of the book. However this meant that where the book was illustrated throughout by monochrome plates, as in *Airplanes*, *Dogs* and *Horses & Ponies*, or when a suitable picture could not at first be found, as in *Geology*, the jacket picture had to be in monochrome too. Their resultant drab appearance might not have mattered much in the monochrome postwar bookshops, when printing inks and paper were still rationed and 'war economy' dust-jackets were still the rule.

In the early 1950s, the old 'Mother Nature' jackets were scrapped, and new all-colour jacket designs lent the series a more uniform appearance. Another improvement was the removal of the word 'British' which left a cleaner, less cluttered design, with simple, often one-word titles like *Ferns*, *Ships* and *Music*. Most of the pictures on the jacket were taken from the body of the book, though there were some odd exceptions. The jacket picture on *Butterflies* was borrowed not from that title, but from *Insects & Spiders*! And to find a coloured Dog, an attractive Cocker Spaniel was found from among the related series of Observer's Picture Cards. The jackets were further brightened up by varying the colours of the title letters from a prevailing green to red, blue, brown or black. Some of these 1950s jackets are very attractive: look at the delicate design of *Ferns* and the harmonious composition of *Railway Locomotives* or *Common Fungi*. They are not just knocked together, but designed with care, and with the fine lettering of a natural craftsman.

Despite all these improvements, the Observer's jackets were beginning to look rather old-fashioned by the end of the 1950s, compared with their increasingly stylish rivals in the bookshop. That the old, ornate, hand-lettered style had lasted so long was due to the conservative influence of Warne's managing director, Dick Billington, who had been

with the firm since the 1920s, and to Bert Stuart's artistic abilities. *Cats* (1959) was the last new title in an old style jacket. In that year *Automobiles* and *Aircraft* appeared in a full-colour photographic jacket for the first time, and when, in 1962, the next two titles, *Sea and Seashore* and *Astronomy*, appeared, they too were clad in photographic jackets, though still with hand-lettered titles. One by one the older jackets were replaced by full-colour ones during the 1960s. This period ushered in what to some are the most attractive Observer's jackets of all –

Thorburn's portrait of robins (adult and juvenile) was a happy choice for the jacket of *The Observer's Book of Birds* in the late 1960s.

the delightful Robin jacket of *Birds*, for example, or the atmospheric jacket of *Weather* – though others regret the replacement of the graphic artist with photography. Unfortunately what had been a uniform series in the 1950s now became a mixture of new and old styles, with a few, like *Music*, *Insects*, *Garden Flowers* and *Cacti*, maintaining their original livery to the end of the decade. Around 1970, some of the jackets were laminated to make them more durable in the shops, producing a surface sheen, known by collectors as 'glossies'.

Uniformity returned with a vengeance in the 1970s. White jackets were back, this time on glossy laminated paper. Each bore a framed colour photograph of identical size, and with similar printed title lettering. The photographs, selected by A.F. Stuart, were usually well-chosen. Less fortunate was the choice of red ink for the title letters, for the red pigment tends to fade in direct sunlight, so that the title on the spine turns ever-paler and can even disappear altogether. Gone now were the individual characteristics of the older books, and in their place were rows of gleaming guardsmen on parade, trim, glossy, stylish, and all the same. They are technically well-designed, but, for the book collector at least, rather boring in their uniformity. In 1979 came the only substantial change of the decade – the replacement of dust-jackets by a cheaper integrated format with laminated boards but bearing the same design as before. This affected all titles still in print as well as new ones. The appearance of cloth was preserved by embossing in a style similar to the previous fabroleen boards. The result was very successful: it produced a neater book than ever, and in most cases preserved the previous dustjacket design. This means that the same design often occurs both as a paper wrapper (1972-79) and a laminated board (1979-85). The same laminated board design was borrowed by the short-lived Australian series.

The hardback Observer's books ceased production in the mid-1980s. When, in 1983, production was switched in the more successful titles to paperback with the New Observer's Books, the wrappers featured a variety of modish, full-colour graphic designs in a slightly enlarged format. Penguin Books redesigned the series in 1987, first in paperback and later in hardback form by subsidiaries. The reprints bore a new design based on a colour photograph, with the Observer's insignia printed along the top edge on a plain background.

While few would claim that the Observer's jackets are significant works of art, they are icons of their period, and were functional and attractive. Taken together they form an interesting example of the wider changes in taste and technical methods employed over half a century of book production. Among our personal favourites are the delightful Robin design of *Birds* (1967), the graceful jacket of *Ferns* (1950), the well-proportioned *Railway Locomotives* (1955) and, in a different way, the powerful Penguin/Bloomsbury *Pond Life* (1992), all of which express the nature of their contents with style and elegance.

Endpapers. From the mid-1950s onwards, many Observer's books were given informative illustrated endpapers, some of which are very imaginative and nearly all of them add to the quality of the book. About 36 titles in the series are so illustrated, some of them acquired during the lifetime of the book, like those of *Horses and Ponies* and *Trees*. Perhaps the most attractive are the woodblocks of *Furniture* which are not only useful for the book (as the only colour in it) but have the decorative quality of marbled endpapers. The Fishing books, and the *Jazz*, *Folksong* and *Big Band* titles contain atmospheric endpapers which create a mood appropriate to their subject. Other endpapers have educational aims. John Clegg used the opportunity to reproduce a field key to pond fauna. Anthony New illustrated *Churches* and *Cathedrals* with architectural drawings, while William Gaunt produced charts showing the development of art down the ages. Of the sports titles, *Cricket* and *Show Jumping* respectively provide a pitch and a course, a useful idea that the other sports titles unfortunately failed to follow. The topographical titles have maps of their respective areas on their endpapers. Patrick Moore, naturally, shows the sky at night. Perhaps more innovative are the world's vegetation and faunal zones in *Zoo Animals*, the seedlings in *Trees*, and the plans for garden borders in *Herbs* (curiously, the herbs themselves appear on the endpapers of *Vegetables*), and also the neatly-drawn twiddly bits in the 1977 *Lichens* and the dinosaur's footsteps in *Fossils*. *Ancient and Roman Britain* illustrates both aspects of its subject with neat maps of Stonehenge at one end and Hadrian's Wall at the other. Other subjects range from silhouetted caterpillars and spacesuits to anatomies of horses and cats and exhibitions of darning needles.

The Lake District deserves special mention since there are two different endpaper designs sharing the same edition. What is apparently the earlier version bears an Ordnance Survey map of the central Lakes, while the other has a toned contour map by John Bartholomew & Sons. Collectors call these '74 Map 1' and '74 Map 2'. The former is much the less common. As trade agents for Bartholomew, Warne perhaps felt it an opportunity to advertise the atlas firm's wares, or maybe be they had forgotten to seek permission from the Ordnance Survey.

'Erin'. In 1989 a special impression of the Penguin paperback *Observer's Birds* was included as part of a birdwatching kit marketed by Erin Marketing Ltd, which also included a seed feeder and a cassette tape of bird songs. The book has a flash in the bottom right corner labelled SPECIAL Erin EDITION. It is already hard to come by as a complete kit, and has its place among Observer's collectables.

Printings of Oberservs Birds commemorating the 50th anniversary of the series and a special birdwatching kit.

'Farnborough 1980'. A limited number of the 1980 edition of *Aircraft* were given a special jacket for the Farnborough air show that year, where complimentary copies were distributed by Henry Wiggin & Co Ltd. The jacket is titled FARNBOROUGH 1980, and depicts the Wright Brothers' aircraft and the air show symbol. Inside, pasted onto the free endpaper, is the Henry Wiggin bookplate. The book is otherwise the standard trade edition. Like the Alcan edition, it is sought after by collectors and worth perhaps £15.

Fellow travellers. A quartet of pocket books by Edward Step called *Nature Rambles* (the 'Come with Me' books) were first published in 1930, and remained in print for three decades. Their questing approach was in the same spirit as the early Observer's nature titles, and, as proof of their kinship, each series advertised the other on its dustjacket. They also share some illustrations, notably the bird paintings by Thorburn, used by Warne over and over again. The attractive jacket printed for *Nature Rambles* in the forties and fifties has the same style of lettering as the contemporary

Two collectable fellow travellers by Edward Step published by Frederick Warne.

Observer's series; and its kingfisher bears a close resemblance to the original *Observer's Book of Birds*. In the same series, and similarly divided by season, were twin volumes by Step on *Nature in the Garden* (1931). Edward Step's style wears well, and these attractive books are not only collected, but, dare one say, even read.

Warne's 'Wayside and Woodland' series must, as we have already seen, be regarded as Observer's fellow travellers *tout court*, and they were regularly advertised on Observer's jackets. Three Observer's titles – *Garden Flowers*, *Flags* and *Heraldry* – were produced in response to popular demand, generated respectively by *The Book of Garden Flowers* by G.A.R. Phillips, *Flags of the World* by H. Gresham Carr, and *Boutell's Heraldry* revised by C.W. Scott-Giles. The Observer's Books of *Flowering Trees & Shrubs* and *House Plants* were essentially abridgements of two titles by the same author, Stanley B. Whitehead: *The Book of Flowering Trees and Shrubs* and *The Book of House Plants*, published over twenty years earlier. See also **Puzzle Books, Young People** and **Zig-zag Books**.

First editions. Most first edition Observer's Books carry the year of publication on the rear of the title page below the copyright details. Generally speaking, if there is no date then the book is not a first edition. First editions can also be identified more reliably from their printer's code (q.v.) by matching them up with the catalogue produced by Mick Burgess. The 'menu' of Observer's titles on the flap also ties the date of the jacket to within a year or two, and more importantly, helps to establish whether or not the jacket is original to the book. First editions are, of course, more valuable in book-collecting terms than subsequent editions, and may cost up to twice as much secondhand. Some of the later titles were only printed once, and so *all* these books are first editions. There are examples in the series where the first edition is in other ways inferior to subsequent ones, notably *Ferns*, which lacks any photographic plates, *Birds' Eggs*, where crude ovals stand in for pale-coloured eggs, or *Birds* which has a dull cover and badly printed pictures. Needless to say, these defects do not affect their collectibility in the least.

Matters are complicated by two examples of a first edition existing in different 'states'. In the short-lived *Basic Aircraft – Military* book, the dustjacket advertises *The Observer's Book of Aircraft* on the back of the jacket, but whereas in one the gap between the two illustrations is blank, in the other, there is an overprint stating 'Previous editions now all sold. Next edition 1968'. Clearly the former state is the earlier and hence the more desirable. Unfortunately it is also much the rarer of the two, and is very hard to find. The second example is *The Lake District* which contains two different sets of endpapers (see **Endpapers**).

Some of the earlier titles were completely rewritten in the 1960s and 70s, often by a different author and with different illustrations. Since the title itself was retained (except *Fungi*, which was changed to *Mushrooms*), these were listed as new editions, not first editions. An exception is the 1980 edition of *The Observer's Book of Weather*, which ignores its predecessor and appears to be a First Edition. And, therefore, since the book says so, it is.

Forewords. A minority of Observer's titles have a Foreword by an eminent personage, whose purpose was to endorse the book, or the author's credentials, or both. Most of the sports titles were endorsed by well-known sporting personalities. In other cases, the Foreword was written by a friend or colleague of the author. An interesting one is the Foreword of *Ships* by W.J. Bassett-Lowke. Though there is nothing in the book to say so, he was chairman of a well-known firm of model makers who built display models for airlines and shipping companies; his endorsement indicated that *Ships* was a useful book for model enthusiasts as well as spotters. Three other Forewords were particularly significant. The endorsement of *Observer's Book of Aircraft* by Peter Masefield, chairman of the Aircraft Recognition Society, reprinted in subsequent editions, helped to establish this book as the standard pocket guide for aircraft spotters. For *Automobiles*, Stirling Moss wrote a different Foreword each year, picking out items of particular interest during the previous twelve months. And for *Bird's Eggs*, the publishers were anxious not to appear to be encouraging nest-robbing (which was shortly to become illegal). They therefore took the precaution of reinforcing the Foreword by P.E. Brown, Secretary of the RSPB (Royal Society for the Protection of Birds) by adding a publisher's note: 'this book has been compiled in the hope that ..... the observer will be content to study eggs and nests in their natural surroundings *– and to leave them there*'.

The full list of Observer's Forewords is as follows:

Birds. The Countess of Warwick (a member of the Bird Protection League, started by the author)

Butterflies (later editions). N.D. Riley (curator of insects at the Natural History Museum)

Grasses. A. Bruce Jackson (a prominent botanist)

Geology. Professor H.L. Hawkins FRS (Reading University)

Aircraft. Peter Masefield (President of the Aircraft Recognition Society, to which the original author also belonged)

Architecture. F.R.S. Yorke FRIBA (a prominent architect)

Automobiles. Stirling Moss OBE

Ships. W.J. Bassett-Lowke FRSA. From 1958, A.C. Hardy, an Oxford professor and President of the World Ship Society

Birds' Eggs. P.E. Brown (Secretary of the Royal Society for the Protection of Birds)

Football. Sir Alf Ramsey

Cricket. Ray Illingworth

Motor Sport. Graham Hill

Show-Jumping. George Hobbs (Chairman of horse show committees)

Jazz. Humphrey Lyttelton

Big Bands. Alan Dell (BBC Producer)

Vintage Cars. Lord Montagu of Beaulieu

Classic Cars. Michael Bowler (magazine editor)

Canals. Sir Frank Price (Chairman of British Waterways Board)

Forgeries. A forgery is a fraudulent imitation made in order to pass it off as the real thing. In the world of twentieth century books, it is the jacket which is most commonly forged. In days gone by, no Observer's Book was valuable enough to be worth forging. Today however, with accurate laser-printed colour photocopiers available, and a healthy collector's market, this may no longer be true. A photocopied jacket is a legitimate standby in a private collection; but if it appears on sale masquerading as the genuine article it becomes a forgery. Usually even the best photocopied jackets can be distinguished from the real thing by a dull (chalky) matt tone compared with the shinier cream original, and lack of any obvious patina of age, but this needs experience. It is a case of 'let the buyer beware'. Observer's collectors are honest souls, and any photocopied jackets are usually labelled as such. But it is something to beware of when seeking rare books, such as the Cyanamids, *Airplanes* or the 1937 *Birds* and *Wild Flowers*. We have not yet seen any examples of a forged *book*, unless you admit *Country Houses* (see **Missing Title**).

'Glossies'. Before the Observer's series switched to new jackets in 1972, some of the old-style jackets were specially laminated. These are easily detected by their glossy sheen; and it doesn't suit them. Perhaps only the last batch were given the glossy treatment and for some titles they are scarce. 'Glossies' have been detected on the following titles: *Birds*, *Wild Flowers*, *Butterflies*, *Horses*, *Geology*, *Aircraft*, *Insects*, *Weather*, *Cacti*, *Flags*, *Sea and Seashore*, *Astronomy*, and *Churches*. They are sought after by the collectors who have acquired everything else.

Guides. The Observer's Guides were a main series spin-off published between 1981 and 1984, and initially priced at between £1.95 and £2.50. They shared the Observer's

Pocket Series logo, but their appearance and subject range is quite different. Judging from their elaborate promotion in 1981, with colour leaflets, showcards, display units and discount offers, Warne entertained great hopes for this series. It was contemporary, practical, down-to-earth, and educational. The slogan for the retailers was 'Warne Means Business – for you'. We discern behind the hype a change of direction, and a change in style, away from Warne's old-fashioned ways. It did not work.

Most of the 22 titles published in 1981 were concerned in some way with painting. The 'Art and Craft Series' listed books on painting materials and techniques, while the 'Where Is It' Series focussed on schools of art, such as British paintings from Hogarth to Turner, or Dutch and Flemish Paintings of the 17th Century. Surprisingly, considering the nature of their subjects, the Guides were issued in rather dowdy covers. Published at the same time were *Let's Make Pottery*, *The Herb Grower's Guide* and *Car Care*, which were no doubt intended to be the first of many such guides on domestic subjects.

Another mini-series that started to appear in 1982, though this time without the Observer's logo, was a course on 'Making Clothes'. The first title began with the basics of *Cutting Out*, while subsequent ones dealt with *Sewing*, *Pressing*, *Fitting*, *Tailoring Techniques* and *Fine Finishing*. A related title, published in 1983, was *Embroidery* by Meriel Tilling, a companion to her *Observer's Book of Sewing*, though in a different format.

The run of 32 Guides ended abruptly in 1984, and their impact was ephemeral. Today they are hard to find in the secondhand market, but they have acquired one or two devotees, and the quality of some of them was well up to Warne's traditional standards.

Illustrations. The Observer's series was made possible by the large stocks of natural history illustrations for which Warne had acquired rights of publication through its previous nature titles, especially the long-running Wayside and Woodland library. With the exception of *Airplanes*, it was not until 1949 that original artwork was commissioned for some of these books. The pedigree of the stock illustrations is fascinating, and in some cases long pre-dates the Observer's series. Those of the first title, *Birds*, derive from an expensive but much-admired Victorian book, Lord Lilford's *Coloured figures of the birds of the British Isles* which came out in instalments between 1885 and 1898. The principal artist was Archibald Thorburn (1860-1935), one of the greatest bird artists of all time, and it is mainly his pictures for the book, which he started to paint in 1887, which graced the Observer's book 50 years later.

The antiquity of these illustrations pales in comparison with the pictures in *The Observer's Book of Wild Flowers*. These were based on the delicate drawings of James Sowerby (1757-1822) who began them as long ago as 1790, to illustrate the celebrated multi-volumed work *English Botany*. So fine was their quality that the work is known as *Sowerby's*

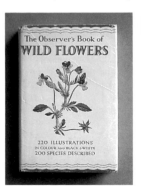

The Observer's Book of Wild Flowers featured coloured drawings originally made by James Sowerby, 200 years ago.

English Botany, though in fact the text was not by Sowerby but by Sir James Edward Smith. The original drawings are in the Natural History Museum, but they have been widely reproduced as engravings, hand-coloured by different artists and printed in many guises, good, bad or indifferent. The Warne art editor had apparently got hold of a copy of one of the nineteenth century editions of Sowerby illustrated by line drawings only, and had probably traced and hand-coloured them for use in Edward Step's *Wayside and Woodland Blossoms*. It was these pictures, duly scaled down and possibly redrawn, which were used in the Observer's Book. Inevitably much of the quality of the originals has been lost in reproduction, and the colouring is relatively crude. But some of the grace and timeless quality of Sowerby's work survives the translation from drawing to engraving to commercial letterpress. When you open OB *Wild Flowers* you are looking at pictures that have been admired and savoured for 200 years.

The original illustrations for *Grasses, Sedges and Rushes* came from a similar source – a nineteenth century of the same *English Botany* with a new text by John Thomas Syme, and hence referred to as *Syme's English Botany*. They were evidently redrawn and coloured by the compiler, W.J. Stokoe. They are attractive enough, but all grasses are green and it has to be said that these pictures do not always look quite like the species they are supposed to represent! This Observer's Book was a strange amalgamation: the pictures borrowed from eighteenth century Sowerby, the text from a well-known Victorian book by grocer's daughter, Anne Pratt, and the whole assembled rather uncertainly by Bill Stokoe, with the help of Bruce Jackson, an elderly expert on tree rings at the Natural History Museum.

The pictures in the Observer's Books of *Butterflies, Trees and Shrubs*, *Wild Animals* and *Larger Moths* were borrowed directly from the parent Wayside and Woodland titles. *Freshwater Fishes* and *Sea Fishes* also borrowed pictures from their Wayside and Woodland counterpart, but their original home was in long out of date and expensive nineteenth century books published in Europe. Thanks to Warne these magnificent fish pictures, which would otherwise have been lost in a few libraries and collections, were brought to a wider public throughout much of the twentieth century.

With *Geology* (1949), Warne began to commission original artwork for its new natural history titles, now being printed in much larger quantities. They were lucky in attracting the services of two excellent illustrators, H.D. Swain and Ernest Mansell. The Surrey-based Mansell's portly build and large hands belied the delicacy of his artwork. His paintings adorned Haslemere Educational Museum in the 1950s, and, fittingly, his work illustrates books written by two curators at that establishment, Arthur Jewell's *Mosses and Liverworts* and John Clegg's *Pond Life*. Mansell also illustrated *Common Fungi*, whose author, Elsie Wakefield, was also associated with Haslemere Museum. It was a shame that Mansell's pictures in his fourth and last Observer's Book, *Sea and Seashore*, were printed by lithography on uncoated paper which failed to do them justice. On the other hand lithography proved a more suitable medium for the subtle colours of bird's eggs, so brilliantly depicted by H.D. Swain in the Observer's Book of that title.

Swain's eggs were, arguably, the high point in the series as far as colour illustration is concerned, at least until the 1970s. From the 1960s, photography and text drawings became the dominant means of illustrating the books, though there were still outstanding contributions to come. The technical standard of some of the later nature artists was very high indeed, notably Ian Garrard's contrasting summer and winter paintings for the 1977 revision of *Trees and Shrubs*, Gordon Riley's coloured drawings in *Caterpillars* and (better still) in the later editions of *Pond Life* and *Insects*, Claire Dalby's for the 1977 revision of *Lichens* and A.D.A. Russwurm's for the 1989 edition of *Butterflies*. Garrard's and Riley's work was also printed and sold in poster form. Another regular illustrator of the 1970s and 1980s was R.B. Davis who specialised in botanical illustrations in colour and line.

Nor must we neglect the often excellent original text illustrations, which began with the litho-printed drawings in *Architecture* made by the authors themselves – a trend continued in the lavishly illustrated *Ships* by Frank Dodman, himself an art teacher by profession. Dennis Punnett's accurate silhouettes for successive editions of *Aircraft* were of an impressive standard, and were later used by some Observer's Directories. Baz East's drawings for the three fishing books of the series (and also *Tropical Fish*) are admirable, as are the neat drawings by Jasper Diamond in *Castles*, Christine Bousfield's in *Show Jumping* and *Pets*, and Anthony New's highly educational pictures in *Old English Churches* and *Cathedrals*. Outstanding among these later titles is *European Costumes* which is illustrated on nearly every page by a most delightful frieze by Pauline Baynes, depicting how men and women have dressed over the past 2,000 years.

Inscriptions are not wanted. Many, maybe most, Observer's Books once owned by a child will carry the name of the proud owner in vast wobbly letters in purple ink, or, alternatively, bear a birthday greeting from Auntie Brenda in biro. *Horses and Ponies* seems especially prone to hideous scribbles. Another common undesirable is the ex-school library book, complete with stamps and dirty fingermarks, of which William Gaunt's art books probably head the list. In terms of collectability, these are serious blemishes, but, in the words of another scribe, 'if that doesn't matter to you, then it simply doesn't matter'. Just occasionally one finds an inscription of real charm or interest. Among our favourites is the copy of *British Birds* inscribed 'For Auntie and the "Tits"' or the 1941 copy of *British Butterflies* with the following note: 'A memoir to our first cross country ramble from Meopham to Cobham since the Blitz of summer 1940. Found incendiaries and craters instead of usual flowers. Bombs dropped Wednesday February 5th.'

Inscribed copies – that is those signed by the author – on the other hand, are very desirable. They seem quite rare – Warne obviously did not organise signing sessions for these books – though John Clegg told us he had signed a great many *Pond Life* in his time. They are likely to be snapped up at a book sale, though not at a great price. On the other hand, signed copies of *this* book are extremely common.

Inserts. In the late sixties and early seventies, the publishers sometimes placed inserts into Observer's books advertising forthcoming titles or related titles. The 1966 and 1971 editions of *Flags*, for example, contained a slip advertising a new edition of *Flags of the World*. In the 1970s, some editions of *Aircraft* carried advertisements for *Air Enthusiasts' International* and its successor, *Air International*, both magazines edited by the author. Inserts in *Jazz* and *Big Bands* advertised record albums to accompany the books and featuring classics described within them – though in fact, apparently because of copyright

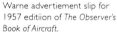

Warne advertisement slip for
1957 ediition of *The Observer's
Book of Aircraft*.

Advertisement slip for *The
Observer's Book of Old English
Churches* (1965).

problems, the albums were never made. *Unmanned Space-craft* (1974) contained a slip behind the end flap advertising the companion *Manned Spacecraft* (but apparently not vice-versa). *London*, *Cricket*, *Zoo Animals*, *Pottery* and *Farm Animals* were other titles advertised by this means. They were not however used for titles with export potential since advertising inserts are illegal in certain countries!

Large print. *The Observer's Book of Music* was printed in quadruple-size for the partially sighted by F.A. Thorpe of Ulverscroft Press in 1965. The book was otherwise identical to the Pocket Series book, apart from the dust-jacket and the lack of colour printing.

Logo. The Warne design mark of a winged horseshoe was never used in the Observer's Pocket Series. In 1977 the series received a symbol of its own in the form of an opened book superimposed on the letter O. It first appeared on the spine of *Vegetables* (1977) and also adorns this book. On *Butterflies* the symbol was accidentally printed upside-down; it seems that no one noticed, since the inverted logo features on all reprints of the book between 1977 and 1985. It might have been suitable for the Australian series, but there the logo is the right way up throughout. Logos were dispensed with for the New Observer's Books, but Penguin Books designed a new one for the series, which appears on both the Penguin and Bloomsbury reprintings. This is a simple 'bulls-eye' made from the initial O of Observers with a dot inside. The idea might have been borrowed from the dotted 'o' in 'Potter' on Warne's Beatrix Potter jackets.

Menu. This is the term used for the list of Observer's titles on the flap of the jacket and opposite the title page. It is useful in helping to establish the approximate date of the jacket, and hence whether or not it matches the book. Buyers should be wary of later jackets wrapped around first edition titles. It is not a crime, but the fact should be noted and the book should not command a first edition price.

Might-have-beens. Suggestions for new Observer's titles – sometimes even whole manuscripts – were a regular feature of Warne's morning mail from at least the 1950s onwards. Sometimes they were from literary agents, touting for their clients, more often from individual enthusiasts insisting on the vast potential of titles on Dolls or Traction Engines. Occasionally an Observer's author, having completed one title, offered another. Among the latter were John Wood-forde's suggestion of *Country Cottages*, Anthony New's of *Stately Homes*, Michael Gibson's of *Greek Mythology* and

Michael Green's of *World War 2 Aircraft*, arranged by country (now *that* would have been nice). Among the more bizarre suggestions came from an American enthusiast who wanted to write an Observer's Book of Motor License Plates. The editor replied, tactfully, that there seemed room for doubt whether this would meet the requirements for a large and continuous demand.

Missing title. The missing book of the Observer's Pocket Series – No. 86 – was to have been *Country Houses*. It was given an ISBN number and advertised in Warne's catalogue.

It was to have provided 'valuable background information' on stately homes, and describe their development and their treasures, plus a county-by-county gazetteer along the lines of OB *Gardens*. Like other contemporary titles, it would have been illustrated throughout with black and white photographs and a block of 8 colour plates.

The contracted author, Patrick (now Sir Patrick) Cormack MP, informed us that *Country Houses* 'was a casualty of the change in the series. I was invited to write the book ..... but at the time the publishers ceased to produce the hardback copies, and changed the policy, my book had not been completed ..... There are, therefore, no copies in existence, to my regret, as well as yours'.

The title that never was. This is a mock-up.

That is not quite the end of the story. In 1994 a member of the Observer's collectors society had 20 mock *Country Houses* made up with blank pages between realistic laminated boards showing how this title *might* have looked! They are the nearest collectors can get to filling that awkward gap on the bookshelf between Nos. 85 and 87.

New Observer's Books. The 25 titles in the 'New' Observer's Books series were in the shops between 1983 and 1986 (see Colour Plate 6). They were in fact mostly the 'old' Observer's books, duly reset and given a facelift with 'bright new covers in modern style', in paperback, or 'flexi-covers' as the advertisers preferred to call it. Market research had shown that 'flexi-covers' were apparently preferred to cased covers, especially by the young, as they were easier to flip open or flip through at the required moment. As the marketing blurb put it, 'the New Observer's Books are designed to meet the requirements of today's reader'. They were only marginally cheaper than the hardbacks, selling in 1985 at £2.50 compared with £2.95. They were also 10% larger than the original series, apparently to suit the American market. Only the more successful titles were reissued in the new format; the others continued to be sold as hardbacks for as long as they remained in print, while *Aircraft* and *Automobiles* (soon to be renamed *Cars*) continued to be revised annually.

Four completely new titles, *Warships*, *Airliners*, *Athletics* and *Tractors* were first published as New Observer's paperbacks. Anthony New's *Stamp Collecting* was another new title, replacing the older *Observer's Book of Postage Stamps*, and now with the emphasis on collecting and printing techniques rather than on design.

The complete list of New Observer's Books is as follows:

N1	1983/84/85/86	Aircraft	William Green
N2	1983/84/85/86	Automobiles	Stuart Bladon
N3	1983	Wild Flowers	Francis Rose
N4	1983/84	Airliners	William Green &
			Gordon Swanborough
N5	1983/86	Warships	Hugh W. Cowin
N6	1983	Cricket	Reg Hayter
N7	1983	Astronomy	Patrick Moore
N8	1983/85	Dogs	Catherine G. Sutton
N9	1983	Tropical Fishes	Neil Wainwright
N10	1984	Horses and	
		Ponies	Jane Kidd
N11	1984/86	Flags	William Crampton
N12	1984	Tanks and	
		Other Armoured	
		Vehicles	Charles Messenger
N13	1984	Athletics	Steve Brennan
N14	1984	Coarse Fishing	Peter Wheat
N15	1984	Fly Fishing	Peter Wheat
N16	1984/85	Soccer	Albert Sewell
N17	1985	British Steam	
		Locomotives	H.C. Casserley
N18	1986	Tractors &	
		Other Farm	Phillip Porter &
		Machinery	Nick Baldwin
N19	1986	Motorcycles	Robert M. Croucher

N20	1986	Ships	Frank Dodman
N21	1986	Pond Life	John Clegg
N22	1986	Stamp Collecting	Anthony New
N23	1986	Castles	Brian K. Davison
N24	1986	Pets	Tina Hearne
N25	1986	Trucks	Nick Baldwin

Pages. If you compare the number of pages in the first 42 titles, you find that they jump all over the place, but that thereafter most titles hold steady close to the average of 192 pages. The actual number of words was more constant than that implies since the shorter books include up to 64 plates which often have their own separate text. From 1972, nearly all Observer's titles were commissioned by the publisher and subject to a contract stipulating length and format. The integrated litho-printing of the later titles, and the reduction of colour, also helped to prescribe the number of pages by reducing the former separation of text and plates. On average, the post-1972 titles have fewer pages than their predecessors. The technical books – *Aircraft*, *Automobiles*, *Railway Locomotives* and *Commercial Vehicles* tend to be among the longer books in the series; the latter title has 312 densely packed pages. At the other extreme are the slim Observer's Atlases of only 120 or so pages.

Penguin

Penguin Observers series published between 1987 and 1991

Aircraft (36th-40th editions, 1987-1992)
Airliners (2nd & 3rd editions, 1987, 1991)
Astronomy (7th edition, 1988)

Birds (Rewritten by Rob Hume)
British Steam Locomotives (revised edition, 1988)
Butterflies (Rewritten by Paul Morrison)
Canals
Cars (30th-35th editions, 1987-92)
Castles
Cats
Coarse Fishing (revised edition, 1989)
Dogs (revised edition, 1987)
Flags (revised editions, 1988, 1991)
Fly Fishing
Horses and Ponies (revised edition, 1987)
Insects
Motorcycles (6th & 7th editions, 1988, 1991)
Pets
Pond Life (4th edition, 1986)
Ships
Stamp Collecting
Tanks (3rd edition, 1987)
Trees
Tropical Fishes
Warships
Wild Flowers

In 1992 and 1993, Bloomsbury Books reissued all of these titles, plus, Cricket, Soccer and Tractors.

In 1992, Bloomsbury also reissued Architecture, Firearms, Glass, House Plants, Rocks and Minerals, Roses, Victoriana and Wild Animals in their original Warne wrappers with Penguin trademark attached.

Photographs. Photographic illustrations are an important feature of most Observer's titles, beginning with *Butterflies* in 1938. As one might expect, their technical quality improved with time, reflecting the vast improvements to cameras, film and printing over the life of the series. Most of the earlier work was in black-and-white. Colour photographs appeared early in the series, but did not approach modern standards of colour printing until the 1960s.

Some of the black-and-white photographs in the early editions of *Trees and Shrubs* and *Ferns* are of historic interest as early examples of outdoor nature photography dating from the turn of the century. The photographers were Henry Irving and Edward Step respectively. The colour pictures of set specimens in *Butterflies* were a remarkable technical accomplishment when they were first printed in the 1900s, while those in *Wild Animals* by Douglas English and others, though mostly studio portraits, and in a few cases probably of dead animals, were among the best available at the time. Some of the latter were taken on black-and-white plates or film, and hand-coloured specially by W.J. Stokoe.

After *Wild Animals*, *Dogs* was the first book to be illustrated throughout by photographs. *Horses & Ponies* followed in similar fashion, as did the books on technical subjects – *Aircraft*, *Automobiles* and *Railway Locomotives*. Of particular interest are photographs taken by the author, some of which were of the highest standards. This trend began with *Insects* (1953) with technically difficult close-ups taken through the microscope of E.F. Linssen. Among other author-photographers were H.C. Casserley (*Railway Locomotives* and *Steam Locomotives*), E.M. Wakefield (*Fungi*), John Clegg (*Pond Life*), Kenneth Alvin (*Lichens*), Noel Lloyd (*London*), Nicholas du Quesne-Bird (*Firearms*), Michael Gibson (*Roses*), John Gagg (*Canals*) and Diana Saville (*Gardens*). Some authors also contributed photographs to other titles in the series; for example, John Clegg's pictures appear in *Seashells* and *Lake District*.

Observer's Picture Cards, sold in bookshops in the 50s and 60s.

Picture Cards. A pack of 32 picture cards might seem an unlikely recipe for commercial success today. In 1953, however, when Warne issued the first 4 sets on subjects covered by its Observer's Pocket Series, the memory of cigarette cards was still recent. Children still eagerly collected picture cards given away with 'sweet cigarettes', bubble gum, packets of tea and cartons of cereal, and learned about aeroplanes or fish or cricketers in the process. For a new generation of young people, Warne began a series of educational picture cards each measuring 4½ x 2½ inches, one side with a full-colour picture and the reverse a panel of 'descriptive text explaining the distinguishing features of the subject'. Their decorative embellishments, too, were reminiscent of pre-war cigarette cards.

The first four sets were I. *British Birds*, II. *Wild Flowers*, III. *British Wild Animals* and IV. *Dogs*, retailing at 2/6 each. They were not joined by further titles until 1962, when five more sets appeared: V. *Domestic Animals*, VI. *Trees*, VII. *Flags*, VIII. *Ships* and IX. *Insects*. *Domestic Animals* was the odd-man-out in that there was no matching Observer's Book title at that time.

At first, the cards were stapled together and perforated.

However in this form they attracted purchase tax, and, since they were printed in three colours, this was at the top rate. Fortunately the publishers found a way out: if bound together at the top edge, the cards were legally defined as books and therefore avoided tax altogether! This was why, from about 1952, the cards were gummed together at the top and given an opaque paper wrapper inside a cardboard packet. Collectors distinguish other variations: in the company name, and whether this is printed on the top or bottom flap.

Curiously enough, except for *Flags* and *Insects*, the Observer's Picture Cards seldom borrow illustrations from the corresponding books. Indeed, it was a Picture Card that was borrowed to illustrate the jackets of *The Observer's Books of Wild Animals* and *Dogs* in the 1950s. Nor did the text coincide. The card descriptions are clearly and simply written, probably by one of the Warne editors, and were evidently intended for the inquiring child of about 7-12.

Products like this can expect heavy use, and it is rare to see a pack today that is not to some degree dog-eared and torn. They were on sale in retail outlets throughout the 1950s and 60s, and were withdrawn from sale around 1970.

Prices. Before the Second World War, Observer's Books were sold at half a crown (2/6 or 12p) each. Some idea of their value for money can be gained by comparing this price with that of average-sized contemporary novels (7/6) or biographies (15 shillings). Warne's Wayside Pocket Guides cost three times as much (7/6) while the Wayside and Woodland Books retailed at between 12/6 and 15 shillings.

War costs forced the price up to 3 shillings, and, during the 1940s, the price of Observer's books crept up by 6d a time, reaching 5 shillings by the onset of the new decade. OB *Geology* came out just after the price-rise to 5 shillings, and so first edition jackets are always clipped, since they

A wartime price sticker. Note the linen bindings showing through the endpapers, characteristic of early Observer's books.

were printed with the old price of 4/6. In the inflation-free 1950s, and well into the sixties, 5 shillings was the standard price of an Observer's Book. It was only with the Sterling Crisis of the later sixties that the price rose first to 6 shillings and then to 7 shillings or 35p at the time of decimalisation.

In the inflationary 1970s and 80s prices rose annually, and Warne were reduced to sending sheets of price stickers to retailers. The almost exponential increase in prices – in line with inflation – can be followed in one of the annually printed titles, *Aircraft*:

Price rises in the Observer's Book of *Aircraft* between 1949 and 1992

Year	Price	Year	Price	
1949	4/6 (23p)	1979	£1.25	
1950-66	5/- (25p)	1980-81	£1.50	
1967-68	6/- (30p)	1982	£1.95	hardback
1968-70	7/- (35p)	1983-84	£1.95	paperback
1971-72	45p	1985	£2.50	"
1973	45-50p	1986	£2.95	"
1974	60p	1987	£3.50	"
1975	75p	1988	£3.95	"
1976	90p	1991-92	£4.99	"
1977-78	£1.10			

The Bloomsbury hardbacks of the early 1990s saw a return to the bargain basement at their remaindered price of £2 or less.

Despite the inflationary prices, which undoubtedly helped undermine the competitiveness of the series, Observer's books have always been good value for money. In 1940, the minimum weekly wage of an agricultural worker would have bought only 10 Observer's Books. In 1960 it would have purchased at least twice as many, and even in the inflationary seventies an Observer's book was only twice the price of an ice cream.

Print-run. During their commercial lifetime, the print-run of Observer's Books was a company secret. Letters in the Observer's archive indicate that at one time not even the authors themselves were told how many books had been printed. No one in this competitive market wished to show their hand to rival publishing companies. With the Observer's series there might have been particular sensitivity since very high sales masked what was in fact a very low profit margin. By the mid-1960s, the cost of paper, printing and binding 'now runs away with the bulk of the money'.

However, on at least one occasion the sales of an Observer's title is revealed in the printed book. According to the *New Observer's Book of Stamp Collecting*, around a quarter of a million copies of its predecessor, *Postage Stamps* (1967) had been sold, an average of 14,000 copies a year during its 18-year life. This is not exceptional for an Observer's Book of that vintage. File evidence indicates that a similar number of copies of *Furniture* were also sold between 1964 and 1982, including some 30,000 during the first year alone. We are told by former Warne employees that printing editions in the 1960s and 1970s averaged about 30-40,000 copies, though the amount did vary from title to title.

Even these figures are dwarfed by the best-sellers of the series. Some 2,855,000 copies of OB *Birds* were printed between 1937 and 1981, and the total by now must be well in excess of 3 million. The fortunes of OB *Aircraft* were equally spectacular – around 2,750,000 were copies printed between 1952 and 1981. For these titles, individual print-runs of 100,000+ copies per year were quite normal, with a record 175,000 of OB *Birds* printed in 1958. The table indicates the sales of the first five titles and Aircraft sold per decade.

Copies sold of selected Observer's titles

Title	First edition	1930s	1940s	1950s	1960s	1970s
BIRDS	20,870	65,870	125,000	870,400	1,040,400	714,200
WILD FLOWERS	20,870	62,430	140,000	512,000	465,700	252,500
BUTTERFLIES	11,820	21,820	61,000	162,650	176,820	148,600
TREES	11,200	31,200	111,640	246,590	358,230	248,600
AIRPLANES	15,000	-	35,000			
AIRCRAFT	20,000 (1949)			971,680	897,400	734,300

An analysis of the annual figures for the first six titles reveals the initially relatively modest sales of Observer's Books before the great leap forward in the 1950s. The small original editions suggest caution – or perhaps inability to invest large sums – on the part of the publishers. The small reprint-runs in wartime and the postwar period probably reflected paper shortages more than lack of demand. During the war, Warne could only reprint titles in alternate years, and even then only in relatively small batches of around 10-15,000. When recovery came in the late 1940s, it was due to two main factors: the ending of paper rationing, and the establishment of a country-wide sales force, calling regularly on all bookshops, station bookstalls and other outlets.

The best selling titles of the series were *Birds*, *Aircraft* and *Automobiles*, followed by *Dogs*, *Horses and Ponies*, *Birds' Eggs* and *Wild Flowers*. Of the later titles, the sales of *Postage Stamps*, *Association Football* (later *Soccer*), *Coarse Fishing* and *Motorcycles* were respectable, reflecting the popularity of these subjects. With a few exceptions, what is noteworthy about all the first 30 or so titles in the series was their *sustained* sales over many years. The pattern begins to change after 1972, especially in the more specialised subject titles. Here one tends to find brisk sales in the first year, followed by a steady but much slower rate thereafter. Some 24,000 copies of *Ancient Britain*, for example, were sold in the first year of publication, but only around 4-6,000 copies in subsequent years. There were still remarkably few unsuccessful titles. *Sculpture*, apparently, was too highbrow a subject for the series, as was *Folk Song*. Fewer copies of *Tennis* were sold than the other sports titles, apparently because most people follow tennis only during the Wimbledon fortnight. More people were interested in Coins than Medals; London and the Lake District proved more popular than the Cotswolds or Devon and Cornwall; and Sea Shells more than Fossils. Oddly enough, there is little correlation between the sales of titles and their relative abundance on the secondhand market today. *Herbs*, for example, is now a difficult title to find, and yet it seems to have sold as well as or better than other Observer's titles published in 1980.

The sales of Observer's Books held steady during much of the 1970s, though, for the older titles, there was a gradual falling-off from previous demand. But in 1980 and 1981, one finds a sudden fall of sales that affected the whole series, even including evergreen titles like *Birds* and *Wild Flowers*. Growing competition, the recession or rising prices may all have been factors, but whatever the reason was, the catastrophic slump in sales must have contributed to Warne's shaky financial position, and the takeover bids of 1982. None of the new titles of 1980-82 reached the usual level of sales of a decade earlier – though it must be admitted that few of them, except perhaps *Tanks*, were likely to enjoy the same broad appeal.

First year sales of new Observer's titles 1972-1981

Cathedrals	23,218	Tropical Fish	18,401
Flowering Trees & Shrubs	25,066	Vegetables	17,846
		Fly Fishing	16,332
Zoo Animals	28,673	Coins	21,479
House Plants	17,782	Sea Shells	17,606
Association Football	44,207	Fossils	12,009
		Pets	23,700
Manned Spaceflight	24,845	Cotswolds	10,796
Cricket	25,344	Lake District	17,988
London	28,232	Firearms	16,372
Pottery & Porcelain	17,549	Jazz	12,022
Unmanned Spaceflight	31,459	Big Bands	12,710
		Castles	15,242
Motor Sports	24,663	Caterpillars	15,345
European Costume	15,520	Rocks and Minerals	13,774
Awards and Medals	14,552	Tennis	8,349
Ancient Britain	23,933	Sea Fishing	12,038
Sewing	17,194	Devon & Cornwall	10,267
Golf	16,481	Roses	13,919
Coarse Fishing	30,048	Herbs	11,809
Show Jumping	22,512	Folk Song	4,936
Motorcycles	44,368	Silver	6,881
Glass	13,458	Tanks	13,635
Tourist Atlas	25,910	Victoriana	5,294
Small Craft	12,082		

Annual sales of selected Observer's titles 1968-81

	1968	1969	1970	1971	1972	1973	1974	1975	1976	1977	1978	1979	1980	1981
BIRDS	95,647	85,197	74,011	61,824	96,854	93,870	95,500	83,939	81,665	66,428	60,438	56,488	45,623	25,344
WILD FLOWERS	36,499	30,560	27,782	28,221	42,865	42,444	28,304	46,977	34,480	28,095	34,463	30,358	24,853	13,756
BUTTERFLIES	15,436	15,393	15,724	11,893	15,816	18,309	19,566	15,653	17,965	13,798	13,503	12,855	10,572	7,293
TREES	27,543	24,533	21,864	22,528	30,874	30,580	191	44,592	31,830	25,113	26,468	20,813	20,550	9,577
WILD ANIMALS	31,295	26,622	22,986	19,068	38,549	29,751	31,151	25,813	24,508	18,260	17,850	17,057	14,886	6,667
GEOLOGY	23,571	20,761	7,597	19,753	17,927	19,769	16,124	17,006	12,355	11,137	8,612	7,768	4,742	3,078
MUSIC	17,225	14,934	12,501	9,710	13,277	13,790	14,113	11,259	11,099	9,886	2,817	16,201	4,971	3,983
WEATHER	16,552	9,821	13,650	9,462	10,386	14,552	14,232	11,697	10,755	11,551	10,760	2,901	13,374	2,544
PAINTING	10,728	8,000	9,282	6,475	7,440	8,984	7,908	795	7,443	3,384	4,421	2,238	34	3,072
ASTRONOMY	25,168	28,357	17,909	21,373	26,430	25,839	26,539	21,167	18,352	15,093	27,048	15,182	14,690	9,443

Printers. The Observer's books were printed for Warne by contractors, of whom the most regular was the old-established printing firm of William Clowes Ltd of Beccles, Suffolk. Clowes had printed the text of many of the Wayside and Woodland titles up to 1950, although the plates were printed separately by Edward Evans Ltd and bound in. The first Observer's books were both printed and bound by William Clowes, and followed the Beatrix Potter books in combining colour pictures and text on the same page. To allow colour printing on text pages, Clowes used a special clay-surfaced art paper, fine-textured enough to reproduce fine detail. The letterpress machine used was a 'Mealy Two-colour' which transferred the image from copper plates pinned to the blocks. Two 'passes' through the machine were needed, the first time to print yellow and black, the second to add red and blue. For that reason, the colour registration had to be exact. It was a job for an experienced printer, who adjusted the setting of the blocks as necessary. The colour paintings reproduced in *British Birds* was a particularly challenging assignment, and sometimes, especially in the early printings, you can see where the registration has slipped slightly, producing separate yellow, blue or red outlines around the image. Technical improvements allowed better reproduction later on, but the results achieved were very creditable given the equipment available in the 1930s, when so much depended on a manual printer's skill.

Another regular printer-binder from about 1950 was Butler & Tanner Ltd of Frome, Somerset. They were given *Aircraft* (from 1951) and *Automobiles*, which required no colour printing, apart from the jackets, but larger-than-average print-runs. One of the first titles to break the mould was *Geology*, which, from 1954, was printed in-house using the London-based Eden Press recently acquired by Warne.

The litho-printed *Music* brought in a new printer, Richard Clay & Co, though *Architecture*, which was printed by similar methods, reverted to Clowes. From the mid-50s, Warne began to shop around more; William Clowes and Butler & Tanner continued to print many titles, but the printer now varied from title to title, presumably in response to particular technical needs or to a competitive tender. By the 1970s, it was becoming common commercial practice to separate the setting and the printing, so that, for example, many titles printed by Clowes were typeset by a firm called CCC. *Football* is of interest as the first title to be printed by filmset, a technique later used for other sports titles. The initial results of filmsetting were poor, especially in *Golf* and *Motorcycles*, which combined indifferent type with microscopic point-size. On the whole, however, the earlier standard of printing was maintained and, in terms of printing illustrations, greatly improved.

The printing contractors used by Warne between 1937 and 1982 were as follows:

William Clowes & Son	38	Richard Clay & Co	2
Butler & Tanner Ltd	22	Taylowe Ltd	2
Morrison & Gibb Ltd	9	Hazell Watson & Viney Ltd	2
Lowe & Brydone Ltd	5	John Bartholomew & Son Ltd	2
Jarrold & Sons Ltd	5	Eden Press	1
Pitman Press	4	W. & J. Mackay & Co	1
Cox & Wyman Ltd	3	C. Tinling & Co	1

Printer's reference code. From 1938, the majority of Observer's Books contain a printer's code or colophon, usually situated either at the end of the book, below the index, or at the rear of the title page. In its original form this was an important source of information, enabling each book to be dated accurately and allowing separate printings to be listed and catalogued. The first part of the code is the printer's own reference number. The second part, separated by a dot, gives the month and year of printing. For example 554.861 indicates that the book was printed in August – the eighth month – 1961. Of course this is not the date of *publication*, for there is binding and retailing yet to be done. Sometimes the book did not appear in the shops until the following year.

Printings. Thanks to the assiduous research of Mick Burgess and other Observer's collectors, each printing of an Observer's title has been catalogued by reference to the printer's reference number (see above). Their number forms an indication of the relative commercial success of each title, though the number of copies per printing varied considerably – and as a general rule print-runs in the 1970s were much larger than those thirty years earlier. Collectors note: the print number does not always conform to a particular dustjacket.

Number of known printings of each title 1937-1985

Birds (1937-85)	50	Ferns (1950-66)	7
Wild Flowers (1937-81)	43	Architecture (1951-81)	15
Butterflies (1938-85)	31	Larger Moths (1952-78)	10
Trees (1938-85)	37	Ships (1952-81)	23
Wild Animals (1938-80)	34	Music (1953-79)	17
Freshwater Fishes (1941-78)	24	Insects & Spiders (1953-78)	15
Grasses (1942-76)	17	Birds' Eggs (1954-81)	18
Airplanes (1942-45)	3	Common Fungi (1954-64)	5
Dogs (1945-80)	35	Mushrooms &Toadstools	
Horses & Ponies (1949-79)	30	(1977)	2
Geology (1949-79)	21	Mosses & Liverworts	
Aircraft (1949-82)	38	(1955-64)	3

Automobiles (1955-82)	27	Basic Aircraft, Military		
Weather (1955-80)	14	(1967-68)	2	
Railway Locomotives		Commercial Vehicles		
(1955-79)	13	(1966-81)	6	
Pond Life (1956-80)	11	Heraldry (1966-80)	5	
Garden Flowers (1957-80)	12	Postage Stamps (1967-79)	6	
Painting (1958-80)	7	Cathedrals (1972)	1	
Cacti (1958-81)	12	Flowering Trees (1972-79)	3	
Sea Fishes (1958-79)	8	Zoo Animals (1972-78)	3	
Flags (1959-79)	7	House Plants (1972-81)	5	
Cats (1959-81)	12	Football/Soccer (1972-80)	5	
Sea & Seashore (1962-77)	8	Manned Spaceflight		
Astronomy (1962-78)	9	(1972-78)	3	
Lichens (1963-77)	3	Cricket (1973-79)	3	
Modern Art (1964-80)	4	London (1973-80)	3	
Furniture (1964-80)	6	Pottery & Porcelain		
Churches (1965-76)	4	(1973-81)	3	
Sculpture (1966)	1	Unmanned Spaceflight		
Basic Aircraft, Civil		(1974)	1	
(1967-68)	2	Motor Sport (1975-78)	2	

From here on, many titles were printed in single edition only. These are omitted. The following titles were printed more than once:

Ancient Britain (1976-79)	2	Tropical Fishes (1976-)	2	
Golf (1975-82)	3	Farm Animals (1976-78)	2	
Coarse Fishing (1976-82)	4	Fly Fishing (1977-80)	2	
Show Jumping (1976-78)	2	Pets (1978-80)	2	
Motorcycles (1976-82)	4	Firearms (1978-82)	2	
Tourist Atlas of GB				
(1976-81)	2			

Puzzle Books. In 1949 Warne published four slim picture books with the unusual basic idea of asking their young readers to label the pictures *themselves* on the basis of various 'clues'. The answers were given on the last page. These were the Puzzle Books, which remained on sale inside their cheerful Ovalteeny wrappers until the 1960s. The titles were The Puzzle Books of Animals, Flowers and Birds by Patricia Baines, and The Puzzle Book of Dogs by Clifford Hubbard (the author of OB *Dogs).* The purpose behind them was essentially the same as the Observer's Books: to encourage children to watch and identify wild animals and plants (and dogs) by looking closely for their distinguishing features. By wrapping it up as a puzzle game, the books provided fun and helped children to become observers in a painless and natural way.

Rarities. While nearly all Observer's titles were printed in large numbers, the survival rate has been very low, and first editions of the early titles are now scarce in collectable condition, especially *Birds, Wild Flowers* and *Freshwater Fishes.* This is also true of *Airplanes* in any edition and the 1949 edition of *Aircraft.* You also need to be very quick to find collectable copies of the annual editions of 1950s or even early 60s *Automobiles,* most of which were confined to a single printing. A full set of *Automobiles* is perhaps the hardest object in Observer Book collecting. More surprising is the short supply of many of the titles published between 1980 and 1982. However these were on sale for only a few years before being remaindered or withdrawn. Other titles already in the rare book category are the Australian series and the special jackets, like Alcan and Cyanamid.

A few dustjackets were confined to a single printing, end have become scarce and highly collectable (see Colour

Plate 4). A good example is the 1954 jacket of *British Butterflies*, which was soon replaced after Warne decided to remove the word 'British' from its Observer's titles a few months later, a decision which meant that the *British Birds' Eggs* jacket, too, had a short life. Other rarities include the 1972 new-style jackets of *Lichens*, *Ferns* and *Common Fungi* which bore a black-and-white photograph. The limited remaining stock of these titles was rejacketed in 1972 - perhaps the non-colour jackets was a cost-cutting measure for titles near the end of their print-life. That of *Common Fungi*, depicting a parasol mushroom, was only discovered in 1998, and at the time of writing, only two copies are known (see Plate 8).

There is only one candidate for the 'Penny Black' of Observer's Books: the first edition of the very first title in its original jacket. It is drab, usually grubby and torn, and it passed in a twinkling of the eye, but everybody wants the 1937 *British Birds*.

Special Offers. In 1972, *The Observer 's Book of Furniture* was offered at a reduced 31p (from 50p) with every can of Min Furniture Polish purchased. The offer, which was advertised in *Homes & Gardens,* drew a disgusted response from at least one bookseller, who pointed out that not only did it contravene the spirit of the Net Book Agreement but lowered the image of books in the eyes of the public. No one thinks the more of anything which is offered at a reduced price, he scolded, and that if Warne insisted on such a course then it would be preferable to give away tins of furniture polish with Observer's Books!

The Warne sales staff took the view that the free publicity resulting from such offers was grist to their mill. But apparently the experiment was not repeated until a decade later when a promotion with a pet food manufacturer, offered copies of *The Observer's Book of Dogs* with a number of can labels. By then, it seems, bibliophiles had become less shockable.

Spine. Until the late 1950s, the Observer's title ran up the spine. Apparently this was the style favoured by Warne's managing director, Dick Billington, who thought they read better that way. He was eventually persuaded by A.F. Stuart and others that the down-spine title – by then in general use – looked even better. For most jackets the change-over from up-spine to down-spine was in 1957 or 1958, though *Insects & Spiders* seems to have been overlooked and carried the up-spine title until 1969. The title on the boards followed suit, but not right away. Most books printed before 1960 continued to use the old style, so that one often finds a down-spine jacket combined with an up-spine book, for example with all printings of *Birds* between 1958 and 1961. From No. 25 *(Garden Flowers)* onwards, all titles, jacket and book, were printed down-spine.

From 1949 onwards, most books carry their series number on the spine of both book and jacket. On a few jacket printings, the number seems to have been omitted accidentally, for example, on the 1958 and 1959 reprints of *Trees and Shrubs*. Between 1960 and 1971, the Aircraft jackets were printed with and without a date on the spine. The latter were apparently intended for the main export markets – the USA, Canada, South Africa and the Far East - which did not take all the annual editions.

Spines are an important ingredient in condition, since it is the part of the book visible at all times. Early Observer's Books are often grubby with a greyish or beige cast, but 1950s and 1960s jackets retain their whiteness and title colours well. The 1970s, on the other hand, will brown in direct sunlight, and the title letters are apt to fade.

Stickers. During the inflationary seventies and early eighties, when prices rose almost annually, Warne resorted to printed labels to stick over the original price. These were attached to the inside flap of the jacket, or the reverse of the cover. These were supplied to the retailer as self-adhesive sheets. The first type, used around 1969, were round labels about 2 cm in diameter, but they were soon replaced by smaller rectangular labels in a variety of format. All bore the publisher's name. They cannot be reliably used to date a book, however, since retailers used them on old stock as well as new.

Price stickers are nothing new. Some of the earliest books bear a 3/- sticker - a price rise of 6d - to include 'Extra War Costs'.

Title changes. Several Observer's books changed their names during their lifetime. The wholesale removal of the word 'British' in 1953 struck a blow for conciseness. *Airplanes* and *Aircraft* are really editions of the same book: the name change was due to the inclusion of helicopters and gliders in the 1949 edition, not the change in author, which followed in 1952. Contrariwise, *Railway Locomotives* became *British Steam Locomotives* in 1974, when diesel engines were omitted. In effect, it changed from a book about current locomotives to one of antique types. Another example of two different titles sharing the same number in the series is *The Observer 's Book of Common Fungi* by Elsie Wakefield, which was replaced in 1977 by the more saleable-sounding Mushrooms, *Toadstools and Other Common Fungi* by W.P.K. Findlay. These are really different books, though they share some of the same pictures. In 1979 *Wild Animals of the British Isles* became plain *Wild Animals* on the jacket but retained the former title on the title page. Another name change confined to

One book or two? Though they share the same series number, the authors and in the case of Fungi, the titles, are different.

the jacket only is *Trees and Shrubs* which became plain *Trees* in 1960. Warne wished to avoid confusion with a new title then being planned called Flowering Trees and Shrubs.

Other significant title changes were *Association Football*, which was changed to *Soccer* in 1978; *Coins* to *British Coins* (1980); *Common Insects and Spiders* to *Insects of the British Isles* (1978) and Automobiles, which at last turned into *Cars* when Penguin reissued the book in 1987.

Translations. The Observer's Books were on display at the Warne trade stand at Frankfurt Book Fair, and various titles have been translated into German, Swedish and French (see Colour Plates). The most translated title seems to have been *Dogs,* which became *Hundar* in Sweden (published by Norstedts of Stockholm, 1947), *Il Libro dei Cani* in Italy (published by Cisalpino, 1949), *Wie hen Ik* in Holland, *Hunde* in West Germany and *El Libros de los Perros* in Spain! *Aircraft is* another title available in several languages. A German annual edition, *Flugzeuge der Welt* has been available in paperback form since the 1950s. The Dutch version is called *Wat is dat voor een vliegting?* and there are similar versions published in French and Swedish. In general it was the less insular Observer's titles, like *Aircraft, Automobiles, Astronomy* and *Dogs* that most interested foreign publishers. Other titles translated into German and published by Feckeltrager Verlag of Hanover between 1964 and 1967 as titles in the Taschenführer ('Pocket Leader') series, include *Cacti* (as *'Kakteen'*), *Horses and Ponies* (*'Pferde und Ponys'*), *Ships* (*'Schiffe'*), *Birds* (*Vögel*), *Freshwater Fishes, Astronomy* and *Insects* (*Insekten*). Later on, a number of titles were translated into German by Delphin Verlag of Munich and Zurich, including *Tropical Fishes* (*'Aquarienfische'*), *Roses* (*Rosen*) and *Flowering Trees and Shrubs* under the cumbrous title of *'Bluhende Straucher und Baume im Garten'*! At least one title was translated into Norwegian – oddly enough it was *Grasses,* published in 1970 in a rather stylish wrapper and entitled *Gras.* There are no doubt many others. If any observant reader has spotted, say, a Chinese *Fungi* or a Swahili version of *Lichens* we would very much like to hear about them.

Young People. For more than a hundred years, Warne has specialised in illustrated educational books for children.

Many of the earlier titles were of a moralistic and sentimental tone, which was still a feature of some of Warne's nature books published before 1939. Wartime paper rationing brought a temporary halt to the flood of educational books, and when, in 1949, paper and ink became freely available again, there was a new emphasis, pioneered by *The Observer's Book of Birds*, on field identification. Warne were among the first publishers to cater for young naturalists, and their output in the 1950s encouraged a generation of enthusiastic pond-dippers, flower-pressers and bird-spotters. We have already considered two of the products of this time – Warne's Picture Cards and Puzzle Books. Warne also published three series of books for young people from the next-door stable to the Observer's series. These were 'Tales of the Wild Folk', the 'Mother Nature' books and the Nature Field Series.

'Tales of the Wild Folk' was aimed at younger children – for the 1950s generation who Listened With Mother, watched Rag, Tag and Bobtail on television and read (or were read) Beatrix Potter. The books presented the story of a wild

Tales of the Wild Folk, another educational series published by Warne, sharing some of the design elements of Beatrix Potter's books and the Observer's series.

animal, bird or insect, blending accurate natural history with a Potterish tale of 'fun and play, danger and escapes'. Some 18 of them were written by Cecily M. Rutley and illustrated in full colour by regular Warne artists, B. Butler, Joyce Davies or Joan Wanklyn. They have titles like 'White Wings – a Butterfly', 'Sweet-Song the Skylark' and 'Grass-hopper Green'. The stories sold at a mere 9d each inside paper covers, though a more durable binding which combined three titles at a time, was available for 3/6. For one of the authors of this book, these were among his first nature books, and are remembered with affection.

The 'Mother Nature' books, whose pictures had been borrowed for the early Observer's jackets, were written in the 1930s, and were still on sale in the 1950s at 4 shillings each. The original quartet by Jane Lucas had been written as long ago as 1931, and their sentimental and maternal style is reflected in the titles – Mother Nature's Babies, Mother Nature's Water Creatures, and, rather delightfully, Mother Nature's Queer Creatures. To these, the ever thrifty W.J. Stokoe had later added four more titles much closer in spirit and content to the Observer's Books he was compiling at the same time: Mother Nature's Wild Flowers, Trees, Birds and Wild Animals.

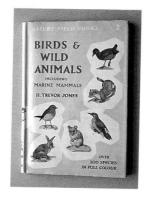

One of four volumes in the Nature Field Series published by Warne in the 1950s.

Yet another nature series of the same period was Warne's 'Nature Field Series', first published in 1952 at 6/6, later reduced to 3/6 each. In these attractive little hardback books, text and colour pictures ran together to provide 'quick easy reference' for the naturalist. As identification guides, their obvious kinship with the Observer's Pocket Series is emphasised by the list of Observer's titles they carry on the rear flap. The brief of the author, H. Trevor Jones, was to cover the whole of British natural history in four volumes. The first, *Wild Flowers,* also crammed in grasses, ferns, fungi and trees, while the fourth was a miscellany of subjects: Shore Life, Fish, Clouds and Weather! The coloured drawings by the regular Warne artist, B. Butler, do not match the standards of nature books today, but they suffice for their purposes. Though more or less forgotten today, the series ran for about ten years and formed a useful introduction to British natural history. There must have been many 1950s children who had their appetite whetted at 4 or 5 by Cecily M. Rutley, Jane Lucas and Beatrix Potter, who moved on to Trevor H. Jones a year or two later and who was collecting Observers by the age of 10. Well, at least one anyway.

Zig-zag Books are a set of 8 books published by Warne in the 1960s. Printed in Italy, they form a series of 48 picture cards joined end to end, and so pull out as a zig-zag. Each card has two illustrations in full colour. The titles are Alpine Flowers and Plants (3 different sets), Freshwater Fishes, Fungi, Minerals, Dogs and Birds.

PART FOUR

BIBLIOGRAPHY AND PRICE GUIDE

This section consists of bibliographical notes on each
Observer's title with pages and illustrations, print life,
number of basic jacket designs, revisions, new editions and
comments. Our price guide for books in excellent condition
is based on recent sales at the book market and auctions
organised by the Observer's Pocket Series Collectors' Society,
and is no more than a guide. The real value of a book will
depend on condition, on the edition and, most of all, on
the demand for it – and demand can vary from year to year,
as will the availability of particular titles. Collectable
Observer's Books should be in tight, clean condition with a
dustjacket, and, except for the oldest titles, will be in Very
Good (VG) or Fine condition. Most titles can be picked up
for less than £5, and poor or jacketless books are worth
very little. For the rarest books the value is in the eyes of
the buyer: prices in excess of £30 may be asked for, but
Observer's collectors are usually, in our experience, fairly
thrifty individuals. Bargains are to be found by those prepared to hunt for them. Prices refer to books sold by Warne
1937-82 in contemporary jackets. Later reprintings are
worth only a pound or two.

Abbreviations

OB = *Mainstream Observer's Pocket Series 1937-1985*
NOB = *New Observer's Book*
PP = *Penguin paperback*
BB = *Bloomsbury Books*

The words British or British Isles were removed from titles 1-7, 10, 12-14 and 17-18 in 1954. The jacket designs are based on the Observer's Book catalogue, *An Observer's Look at Observer's Books*. Available through the Observer's Pocket Series Collector's Society, it contains details of all printings and illustrates all jacket variations.

1. British Birds by S. Vere Benson, 1937

224 pp. 200 illustrations in colour and black & white by Archibald Thorburn and others. 1937 to date. 11 OB jacket designs, PP (4) & BB. Originally covered 226 species, with notes on appearance, haunt, nest, eggs, food and call notes. Revised 1952, 1956, 1960, 1965, 1972. Rewritten by Rob Hume 1987. The excellent illustrations and concise format of one bird per page made this book an enduring classic. With only minor changes, it was in print for half a century, and over 3 million copies were sold.

The early (pre-1954) editions of OB *Birds* are very difficult to find in collectable condition. The first edition is a rare book much in demand but rarely seen. A colour photocopied jacket is an acceptable substitute, and potential buyers should check jackets carefully. A first edition in a VG original jacket was recently sold at auction for £100! Jacket 2 (1937-39) is also elusive in collectable condition. Later editions £1-5, with a premium on VG/Fine examples of pre- 1955 jackets.

2. British Wild Flowers, compiled by W.J. Stokoe, 1937

224 pp. 200 illustrations in colour and black & white, reproduced from *Sowerby 's English Botany* and hand-coloured. 1937 to date. 9 OB jacket designs, NOB, PP, BB. Originally covered 236 species with botanical descriptions and notes on flowering period, habitat and distribution.

Revised 1963, 1965, 1975. Rewritten by Francis Rose with 116 full-colour new illustrations by R.B. Davis, 1978, and in new format 1983. The original book was based on Edward Step's *Wayside and Woodland Blossoms,* and was creaking badly by the 1960s. The Rose revision contains a better selection of common plants, but the original book still has its charms. 1,475,000 copies sold 1937-81.

Like OB *Birds,* the first edition is rare and sought after. A copy in a battered jacket was sold recently for £25. Other printings from 1930s about £10-15; later printings £1-5. A particularly attractive set of jackets, and nice copies of pre-1955 books are elusive.

3. **British Butterflies**, compiled by W.J. Stokoe, 1938
192 pp. 154 illustrations in colour and black & white, reproduced from Richard South's *Butterflies of the British Isles.* 8 OB jacket designs, PP, BB. Covered all British species and their life cycle. Revised 1951 (to include the recently discovered New Clouded Yellow), 1960 with new colour illustrations by H.D. Swain, minor changes 1973, 1977, 1979. Rewritten by Paul Morrison 1989, with excellent new colour illustrations of all life stages by A.D.A. Russwurm (wrongly stated to be 'copied from F.W. Frohawk originals' on the cover). Butterflies were the perfect subject for an Observer's book. Earlier editions emphasised collecting; later ones conservation and attracting butterflies to the garden, but otherwise few changes were necessary. 575,000 sold 1938-81.

The first edition is elusive and usually grubby: £10-15. Later editions £1-5 except the short-lived 1953 'British Butterflies' (Jacket 3) which at auction recently went for about £15.

4. Trees and Shrubs of the British Isles, compiled by W.J. Stokoe, 1938
240 pp. 177 illustrations in colour and black & white, text and pictures based on Edward Step's *Wayside and Woodland Trees*. 1938 to date. 8 OB jacket designs, PP, BB. Described 106 native and widely planted species. Revised with new colour plates 1960, as *Trees*; rewritten 1975 by Herbert L. Edlin, with fine new colour illustrations by Ian Garrard (also available as wall charts). Revised 1985. The earlier versions were rather poorly illustrated but the 1975 Edlin/Garrard edition is a fine book. About a million copies sold 1938-81.

First edition is scarce and worth £10-15 in VG condition. 1930s and 1940s printings around £5-10, later ones £1-5. Jacket 6 (1969-72) illustrating a Horse Chestnut was short-lived and confined to a single printing.

5. British Wild Animals, compiled by W.J. Stokoe, 1938
224 pp. 72 illustrations in colour and black & white. Text based on Edward Step's *Animal Life of the British Isles*. 1938 to 1980. 8 OB jacket designs, BB. Described all 69 species of wild mammals, reptiles and amphibians, illustrated with a mixture of photographs and paintings. Revised by Maurice Burton 1957 and rewritten with new illustrations 1971. In terms of information and pictures, the Burton 1971 edition is much the better book.

First edition is scarce and worth £10-15 in VG condition. 1930s and 1940s printings upwards of £5 but tricky in VG/F condition, later ones £1-5. Jacket 3 with stag combined with 'British Wild Animals' was short-lived, confined to 1953.

6. Freshwater Fishes of the British Isles by A. Laurence Wells, 1941

153 pp + 6 pp blank 'notes'. 76 illustrations in colour and black & white. 1941 to 1978. 6 OB jacket designs. Described 82 species with notes on habits, distribution and angling quality. Revised 1952; rewritten by T.B. Bagenal 1970. The excellent original plates lasted the lifetime of the book. Original author's style is discursive; reviser is crisper, more scientific and more informative.

First edition is very scarce, perhaps £15-20 in VG condition. Later printings £1-6, but Jacket 5 (author T.B. Bagenal in the 'perch jacket') was short-lived (1970-72) and is scarce.

7. British Grasses, Sedges and Rushes, compiled by W.J. Stokoe, 1942

224 pp. 104 illustrations in colour and black & white, reproduced from *Syme's English Botany* and hand-coloured. 1942 to 1976. 4 OB jacket designs. Described 100 species, with notes on names, pasture value and other commercial use. Revised by A. Laurence Wells 1947, and more thoroughly by Francis Rose 1965, 1974. Never a really satisfactory title, as the illustrations were not up to the task of identifying these difficult plants.

First edition is scarce – £10, later printings £1-5. The 'meadow jacket', Jacket 3 is particularly attractive.

Airplanes by Joseph Lawrence, 1942

192 pp. 321 illustrations (photographs and silhouettes)

describing 108 'airplanes'. Revised with additions, 1943 and 1945. The title was un-numbered. Though much sought after for its vintage World War 2 aircraft, the spotter's notes are brief and amateurish compared with the William Green books that followed. A fine copy is every collector's dream. About 35,000 sold.

Very scarce, and usually in poor condition. A good copy in a jacket would be worth at least £35 in any printing. Beware of colour photocopies.

8. Dogs by Clifford L.B. Hubbard, 1945

224 pp. 148 black &: white photographs. 1945 to date. 10 OB jacket designs, NOB, PP (2 jackets), BB. Originally described 300 breeds and varieties with notes on origin, uses, habits and vital points. Regularly updated with replacement photographs. Major revision by Sonia Lampson 1966. Rewritten by Catherine G. Sutton 1978. New format with colour illustrations 1983. Always a popular and concise title, *Dogs* has been translated into five languages.

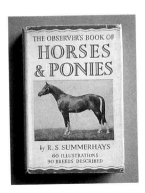

Older printings elusive in collectable condition. First edition £15, the attractive jackets 3 and 4 about £10, others £1-5.

9. Horses and Ponies by R.S. Summerhays, 1949

240 pp. 60 black & white photographs (later increasing to 85). 1949 to date. 10 OB jacket designs, NOB, PP,

BB. Originally described 90 breeds with notes on history and origin, use, breeding and description. Regularly updated and expanded with replacement photographs. New edition revised by Daphne Machin Goodall, 1978. Rewritten by Jane Kidd with new colour photographs, 1984, revised 1987. Another popular title, similar to *Dogs* in arrangement, that kept abreast of developments, with the help of ever-improving illustrations.

Older printings elusive in collectable condition. First edition £5, others £1-5. Jacket 5 ('82 illustrations') was confined to a single printing in 1961.

10. British Geology by I.O. Evans, 1949

266 pp. 182 illustrations in colour and black & white; original line drawings by R.B. Fuller and A.F. Stuart. 1949 to 1979. 5 OB jacket designs. Revised with additional colour plates 1952, and more thoroughly in 1971 with many new photographs. A 'handy little book', written with the zest of an amateur enthusiast and emphasising field observation.

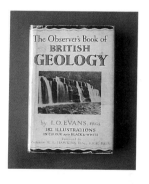

First edition difficult in collectable condition, about £10. Other printings £1-5. Jacket 4 (all-colour 'old man of the moor' rock formation) was confined to 1971-72 and therefore scarce.

11. Aircraft by Joseph Lawrence 1949; by William Green and Gerald Pollinger 1952-60; by William Green from 1961

New edition 1949 replaced Airplanes with new title of Aircraft. 256 pp describing 109 types of airplanes, seaplanes, helicopters and gliders with help of black & white photographs and 3-view silhouettes. From 1952, annual editions edited by William Green with new dustjacket and much-improved silhouettes by Dennis Punnett. 1949 to date. 31 OB annual jacket designs, 4 NOB, 5 PP, BB. Annual revisions and good data established this book as the best cheap up-to-the-minute guide available, and the *vade mecum* of every keen aircraft spotter. Around 100,000 titles a year sold. 2,796,000 sold 1957-81.

Annual editions. Jacket 1 (1949) is scarcest at £15. 1950s jackets £5-10, later ones £1-5. Early editions can be hard to find in acceptable condition.

12.   British Ferns compiled by W.J. Stokoe, 1950

128 pp. First edition had 36 colour plates and line drawings, augmented in 1951 new edition by 36 black & white photographs. 1950 to 1972. 6 OB jacket designs. Described 45

species, with notes on description, habitat and life-history. New edition with more plates 1951, revised by Francis Rose 1965. The title was re-jacketed in 1972 but soon went out of print. An attractive book, thanks to the colour plates, borrowed from a Victorian fern book. The original jacket perhaps wins the series prize.

First edition £10, others

£1-5 **except the** short-lived Jacket 6 (1972) with a black-and-white photograph, which sold at auction recently for £15 in VG condition.

13. British Architecture by John Penoyre and Michael Ryan, 1951

218 pp. 270 line drawings by the authors, some colour over-printed by litho. 1951 to date. 8 OB jacket designs, BB. Described development in buildings from Saxon times to the present followed by a comprehensive 'visual index'. New edition 1954, revised 1958, 3rd edition reset 1975. A well designed pocket encyclopaedia written by professional architects versed in the functional school of the 1930s.

First edition £5-10, others £1-5. Jackets 3 and 4 and virtually identical, but one has full shading on the lawn while the other, earlier, version is almost bare. This may be simply a printing variation.

14. Larger British Moths by R.L.E. Ford, 1952

224 pp. 196 illustrations in colour and black & white, reproduced from Richard South's *Moths of the British Isles.* 1952 to 1978. 5 OB jacket designs. Described 113 species, with notes on life history, collecting end breeding. Revised with new colour illustrations by H.D. Swain 1963; further revised 1974. Arrangement similar to *Butterflies,* but with an original (and excellent) text.

First edition £5-10, others £1-5.

15. Ships by Frank E. Dodman, 1952

192 pp. 221 illustrations in colour and black & white. 1952 to date. 11 OB jacket designs, NOB, PP (2 designs), BB. Originally described over 100 types of ship, ancient and

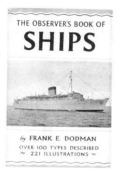

THE OBSERVER'S BOOK OF
SHIPS
by FRANK E. DODMAN
OVER 100 TYPES DESCRIBED
221 ILLUSTRATIONS

modern, from harbour craft to ocean liners, with colour plates of ensigns and flags. Revised and updated regularly; new editions 1953, 1958, 1973, 1981, 1986 with considerably more differences between editions than is normal in the series. 1973 edition was virtually a new book. A lavishly illustrated book with silhouettes, drawings, watercolours and shipping colours, mostly by the author, an art teacher. The 1981 cover depicts the ill-fated 'Herald of Free Enterprise', which capsized with heavy loss of life a few years later.

First edition £5-10, others £1-10.

16. Music by Freda Dinn, 1953

190 pp. 200 illustrations by Paul Sharp, some colour overprinted by litho. 1953 to 1979. 3 OB jacket designs. Described 'Sound and How We Hear It', ancient and modern musical instruments, musical terms and notes on lives of composers. Revised edition 1959, new edition with new illustrations 1979. Large print edition 1965. A pocket encyclopaedia by a professional music teacher in school room style; it has required relatively little updating. The original text in the same jacket remained on sale for twenty years.

All editions £1-5.

**17.   Common British Insects & Spiders by E.F. Linssen &
L. Hugh Newman, 1953**

128 pp. 64 colour and black & white plates, colour artwork
by L.G. Goodwin and A.F. Stuart,
photographs by E.F. Linssen.
1953 to date. 6 OB jacket
designs, PP, BB. Covered all 21
orders of insects, plus representative spiders, describing and
illustrating over 200 species.
Revised 1964. New edition 1978,
retitled *Insects* by Linssen alone,
reset 1987 with new illustrations
by Gordon Riley and new photos
by author. Newman contributed
the original sections on caddis
flies, butterflies and moths.

First edition £5-10, others £1-5. The first four jacket
types are distinguished mainly by the colours of title letters
and scalloped margin.

18.   British Birds' Eggs, compiled by G. Evans, 1954

218 pp. Described eggs of 180 species, illustrated in colour
or outline by H.D. Swain. 1954 to 1981. 3 OB jacket designs.
A companion to OB *Birds,* covered nearly all nesting birds,
with notes on nests, clutch size and distribution. The first
edition was short-lived, and was revised in the same year,
1954, with tinted illustrations for pale or unmarked eggs
in place of the original crude outlines. The lithographed
illustrations were very fine, and this was a popular title
despite prohibitions on collecting.

Scarce first edition with 'British Birds' Eggs' jacket £10.
Others £1-5.

19. Common Fungi by E.M. Wakefield, 1954

118 pp. 32 colour plates by Ernest C. Mansell and 32 black & white photographic plates taken by author and others. 1954 to 1964; reset, retitled and re-written 1977 (revised 1978) as *Mushrooms, Toadstools and other common fungi* by W.P.K. Findlay. 3 OB jacket designs. Described a selection of common or easily recognised fungi with notes on collection, habitats, classification and edibility.

This is really two books. First edition 1954 £5- 10. First edition 1977 is scarcer – £ 10. Only two copies of Jacket 3 with a black-and-white picture of a parasol mushroom were known at the time of writing.

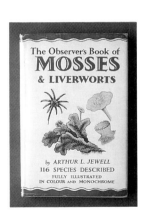

20. Mosses & Liverworts by Arthur L. Jewell, 1955

128 pp. 64 colour and monochrome plates by Ernest C. Mansell. 1955 to 1964. 1 OB jacket. Described 116 common and conspicuous species with notes on classification, habitats and life history. A brave attempt at introducing these difficult plants to 'the weekend naturalist'. Similar in arrangement to *Common Fungi*. A short-lived title with only 3 printings.

All printings £10.

21. Automobiles edited by Richard T. Parsons 1955-56; edited and revised by L.A. Manwaring 1957-69; compiled

by the Olyslager Organisation 1970-79; by John Blunsden 1980-82, by Stuart Bladon 1983 to date. Retitled *Cars* in 1987.

Originally 286 pp, describing 107 manufacturers and 260 models with monochrome photographs and sketches. Like OB *Aircraft*, this book is revised and updated annually and so always contains the latest models and developments. 25 OB jacket design (see Plate 2) 4 NOB, 6 PP to date. Reference book on recognition features, also describing how a car works, company history and models of cars worldwide. The earlier editions contained line drawings for identifying cars by their radiators. The best-selling Observer's Book after Birds and Aircraft.

Nearly all the annual editions were a single printing. The 1955-60 and 1963 editions all scarce and often grubby, so £10-20 in collectable condition. 1960s editions around £10, others £1-5. There is also a rare 1955 American edition.

22. Weather by Reginald M. Lester, 1955

152 pp. 64 colour and black & white plates. 1955 to 1980. 5 OB jacket designs. Describes all aspects of weather forecasting, recording and study 'for the amateur observer'. Revised 1964. New edition, rewritten with new illustrations, many in colour, by Robert Pearce 1980. This is effectively a new book with a different approach. The well-illustrated Pearce book had an undeservedly short run.

All editions £1-5.

The Observer's Book of
WEATHER

By REGINALD M. LESTER, F.R.Met.Soc.
ALL ASPECTS DESCRIBED
FULLY ILLUSTRATED
IN COLOUR AND BLACK & WHITE

23. Railway Locomotives of Britain by Ernest F. Carter
1955; edited by H.C. Casserley 1957-66. Re-titled *British Steam Locomotives* by H.C. Casserley 1974-1989. Illustrated by black & white photographs, from 1957 taken by H.C. Casserley. The first edition only had 8 colour plates by Kenneth E. Carter. 8 OB jackets (see Plate 3), NOB, PP, BB. New editions 1957, 1958, 1960, 1962, 1964, 1966. *Steam Locomotives* 1974 was effectively a new book about antique locomotives as opposed to current ones. It was revised in 1985 and 1988. The Carter book was dry as a bone, with rather poor half-tones. Casserley's had more bounce, and better pictures. A particularly attractive set of jackets.

Scarce first edition £10, others £1-5.

24. Pond Life by John Clegg, 1956
128 pp. 32 colour and 16 black & white plates by Ernest C. Mansell; 16 photographs by author. Illustrated end-papers. 1956 to date. 4 OB jacket designs, NOB, BB (2). Compact pictorial guide to plant and animal life in ponds. New editions 1967, 1980, reset with new artwork by Gordon Riley and Eric Holloway (rotifers), 1986. A classic, perhaps the most successful natural history title after *Birds,* it was first devised as a companion to the author's *Freshwater Life of the British Isles.*

All editions £1-5.

25. Garden Flowers, compiled by Arthur King, 1957
240 pp. 100 colour and 100 half-tone illustrations by Joan Lupton, reproduced from *The Book of Garden, Flowers.* 1957 to 1980. 4 OB jacket designs. Described flowers suitable for average gardens, with notes on planting, cultivation and propagation. New edition 1974 by David Pycraft. Reverted to the earlier approach of boiling down a larger

volume to Observer's size. It was also the first book aimed mainly at the adult market.

All editions £1-5. Jacket 2 (1969 edition) was short-lived (1969-72) and therefore scarce.

26. Painting and Graphic Art by William Gaunt, 1958

160 pp. 16 colour plates and 57 monochrome reproductions. Illustrated endpapers. 1958 to 1980. 2 OB jacket designs. A pocket guide to art appreciation, exploring different schools, themes and painter biographies. Revised 1959. A remarkably wide-ranging but concise pocket companion for visiting picture galleries, aimed at the older school student and general reader.

All editions £1-5.

27. Cacti and other Succulents by S.H. Scott, 1958

160 pp. 64 plates of colour and black & white photographs, mostly by the author. 1958 to 1981. 3 OB jackets. Describes common or easily cultivable cacti, with notes on cultivation and propagation. This title stayed exactly the same, apart from a jacket change in 1972, until 1980. 2nd edition 1981 with new illustrations, revised by J.W.P. Mullard. Perhaps the first title aimed at the *adult* collector.

All editions £1-5. The 1981 (Jacket 3) is the rarest.

28. Sea Fishes by A. Laurence Wells, 1958

160 pp. 64 plates in colour and black & white. 1958 to

The Observer's Book of
SEA FISHES
T. B. BAGENAL

1979. 3 OB jackets. Describes 164 species of saltwater fish with notes on life history, habits and fisheries. Revised 1959. Rewritten 1972 by T.B. Bagenal. The 1972 Bagenal version is a model of concise writing and one of the best natural history books in the series. The original illustrations were good enough to last the lifetime of the book.

All editions £1-5.

29.   Flags by I.O. Evans, 1959

208 pp. 80 colour plates and 74 line drawings. 1959 to date. 5 OB jackets, NOB, PP, BB. Described over 400 national flags, badges, signal codes etc emphasising identification and historic development. Revised 1963, 1966, 1971, 1975. New edition rewritten by William Crampton 1979, revised 1984, 1986, 1988, 1991. Originally based on *Flags of the World* by Gresham Carr. *Flags* has always been a popular title, kept up-to-date by regular revisions and new illustrations.

All editions £1-5.

30.   Cats by Grace Pond, 1959

160 pp. 32 colour and 25 black-and-white photographs, and text drawings by H. Worthington. Illustrated endpapers. 1959 to date. 3 OB jackets, PP (2 jackets), BB. Comprehensive guide to pedigree breeds and pet care Revised editions 1965, 1975. Reset with new illustrations 1979. 4th edition

1987, revised 1991. Another successful title, continuously updated over 30 years.

All editions £1-5.

31. Sea and Seashore, edited by I.O. Evans, 1962

254 pp. 64 plates in colour and black & white, mostly by Ernest C. Mansell. 1962 to 1977. 2 OB jackets. Described the geography – tides, currents, cliffs – and wildlife of the sea and the shore around Britain. Reprint with corrections 1977. This book was printed by lithography, and lacks the illustrative sparkle of its predecessors. A book devoted wholly to shore life might have been more successful. About a quarter of a million sold.

All editions £1-5.

32. Astronomy by Patrick Moore, 1962

222 pp. 64 colour and black & white plates and text star-maps. Illustrated endpapers. 1962 to date. 3 OB jackets, NOB, PP, BB. Litho-printed pocket guide for the naked-eye observer – stars, constellations, moon, sun and planets. Revised regularly, 7th edition 1988. Very concise, and aimed at the observer in Australia as much as in Britain. A fine book.

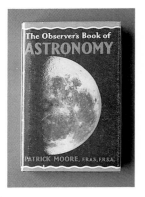

All editions £1-5, but a good first is elusive – the red spine lettering is prone to fading.

33. Lichens by K.A. Kershaw and K.L. Alvin, 1963

126 pp. 64 coloured drawings and black & white photographs by authors. 1963 to 1977. 3 OB jackets. A compact pictorial guide to the commoner and more conspicuous lichens with notes on reproduction, habitats and examination. Rewritten in 1977 by Kenneth Alvin and Francis Rose, with excellent new illustrations by Clare Dalby. This is the best beginner's guide to lichens available, and one of the best nature titles in the series. About 60,000 of 1977 edition sold.

All editions £3-6 except the 'black and white' Jacket 2, used to rejacket the last few copies of the 1966 reprint in 1972. This is very scarce and likely to fetch at least £15 at auction in VG condition.

34. Modern Art by William Gaunt, 1964

148 pp. 16 colour plates and 52 monochrome reproductions. Illustrated endpapers. 1964 to 1980. 2 OB jackets. A gallery visitor's guide to paintings from 1880 onwards. Reprinted but never revised. A companion to *Painting and Graphic Art* in similar format, exploring the various schools of modern art in England, Europe and America. About 115,000 sold.

All editions £1-5.

35. Furniture by John Woodforde, 1964

224 pp. 195 line illustrations. Coloured endpapers. 1964 to 1980. 2 OB jackets. A guide to antique furniture for on-the-spot reference. Revised 1967. Rather a drab book, illustrated only by line drawings (apart from attractive coloured woodblock endpapers), and itemising furniture by period, one by one. About quarter million sold.

All editions £1-5.

36. Old English Churches by Lawrence E. Jones, 1965

214 pp. 4 colour plates and 44 plates of black & white photographs; text drawings and endpaper by later Observer's author A.S.B. New. 1965 to 1976. 2 OB jackets. Visual guide to church architecture and interiors. Revised 1969. Though confined to pre-Reformation churches, this is a splendid pictorial guide to church features, and one of the inspiring books of the series. About 200,000 sold.

All editions £1-5.

37. Sculpture by William Gaunt, 1966

132 pp. 8 colour plates and 62 monochrome reproductions; text maps; illustrated end-papers. 1966-72. Single printing but 2 OB jackets. Companion to author's *Painting* and *Modern Art* and similar in treatment, exploring world sculpture from early times to present day. The relatively brief shelf life suggests the subject was too esoteric for the series, despite the eye-catching jacket and the excellence of William Gaunt's writing. About 30,000 sold.

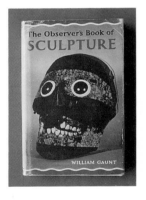

Rather scarce, especially in the replacement Jacket 2 after 1972. £5- 10.

38. Basic Aircraft - Civil compiled by William Green, 1967

272 pp. Illustrated by black & white photographs and 3-

view silhouettes by Dennis Punnett. 1967-68. 1 OB jacket. Compact reference source for basic types of widely-used civil aircraft, supplementing OB Aircraft, which is confined to the latest types and prototypes. In 1974, this book was superceded by the *Civil Aircraft Directory*.

Rather scarce, £5-10, more in 1st state (see First Editions).

39.   Basic Aircraft – Military compiled by William Green, 1967

272 pp. Illustrated by black & white photographs and 3-view silhouettes by Dennis Punnett. 1967-68. 1 OB jacket. Compact reference source for basic types of military aircraft. In 1974, this book was superceded by *the Military Aircraft Directory*.

Rather scarce, £5- 10, more in 1st state (see First Editions).

40.   Commercial Vehicles edited by L.N. Manwaring, 1966; compiled by the Olyslager Organisation 1971-74; compiled by Nick Baldwin 1978-81. Originally 312 pp, illustrated by 344 half-tone photographs and maker's badges. 1966-81. 5 OB jackets. Companion to *Automobiles* with similar layout, describing trucks, vans, buses and other commercial road vehicles worldwide. New editions 1971,1978,1981. About quarter million sold. In 1986 this title evolved into the NOB title, *Trucks* by Nick Baldwin, reprinted in PP and BB.

The rather scarce First edition £5-10, others £1-5.

46. House Plants by Stanley B. Whitehead, 1972

192 pp. 150 colour illustrations by Joan Lupton. Based on the author's *Book of House Plants* – a concise guide to 150 indoor plants, with notes on choosing, growing and propagating house plants. 1972 to 1981. Reprinted BB 1992. Similar format to *Flowering Trees and Shrubs.* About 165,000 sold. £3.

The Observer's Book of
HOUSE PLANTS
STANLEY B. WHITEHEAD

47. Association Football by Albert Sewell, 1972

192 pp. 16 colour plates and 42 black & white illustrations. 5 OB jackets, 2 NOB designs, PP, BB. Guide to football league clubs, championships, footballer biographies, and match records. 1972 to date. New editions 1974, 1976, 1978, 1980, 1984. Retitled *Soccer* in 1978. From 1978 revised by Alan Hughes. One of the most successful latterday titles despite microscopic print. The colour section was devoted to football jerseys.

First edition £4, others £2.

48. Manned Spaceflight by Reginald Turnill, 1972

192 pp. 8 colour plates and over 70 black & white illustrations. Illustrated endpapers. 1972 to 1978. 3 OB jackets. Reference guide to manned space vehicles and their launchers, and astronaut biographies. New editions 1975,1978. Concise account of a then exciting subject. About 165,000 sold.

First edition £4, others £2.

49. Cricket by Peter Smith, 1973

182 pp. 8 colour and 8 black & white plates. Illustrated endpapers. 1973 to date. 3 OB jackets, NOB, PP, BB. Guide to county and world cricket, with sections on cricketing personalities and records. Revised editions 1976, 1979, 1983. Format along the lines of *Soccer*. Colour section on cricketing badges and ties. 120,000 sold to 1981.

First edition £4, others £2.

50. London by Geoffrey Palmer and Noel Lloyd, 1973

192 pp. 8 colour plates and 83 black-and-white photographs by authors; line drawings by Roger Harris. Map endpapers. 1973 to 1980. 2 OB jackets. Historical and architectural guide to London landmarks. Revised 1980. Well constructed travel guide, setting format for later travel titles, coupling historical overview with a gazetteer. About 110,000 sold. £3.

51. Pottery and Porcelain by Mary and Geoffrey Payton, 1973

192 pp. 8 colour plates and 123 half-tones photographs by Shirley Hartshorne, and line drawings. 1973 to 1981. An A to Z of pottery collectables, emphasising the affordable. Set the format and standard for a series of titles aimed at the amateur collector and habitue of museums and stately homes. 87,000 sold. £4.

52. Unmanned Spaceflight by Reginald Turnill, 1974

192 pp. 8 colour plates and over 50 half-tones. Illustrated

endpapers. Single printing, superceded by the author's *Spaceflight Directory*. Companion volume to *Manned Spaceflight,* on spacecraft and launchers of space, moon and planets. 57,000 sold. It ought to be rarer than it is. £5.

53.   Motor Sport by Graham Macbeth, 1975

192 pp. 59 black & white photographs and 39 racetrack diagrams. 1975 to 1978. 2 OB jackets. 'Complete story of motor sport told in a simple style' with details of racing cars, drivers, circuits and championships. Revised 1978. About 80,000 sold. £3.

54.   European Costume by Geoffrey Squire and Pauline Baynes, 1975

192 pp. Line illustrations by Pauline Baynes. Single edition and OB jacket. 'A lively visual cavalcade of changing fashions in European dress between the first century AD and 1900.' A perfect marriage of scholarly text and delightful illustrations. About 35,000 sold. Still surprisingly common. £5.

55.   British Awards and Medals by Edward C. Joslin, 1974

192 pp. 8 colour plates by Michael Tregenza and 186 half-tone illustrations. Single edition and OB jacket. Authoritative ready reference to British orders, decorations and medals. Colour section was on medal ribbons. Note the return of 'British'. About 55,000 sold. £4.

56.   Ancient and Roman Britain by Harold Priestley, 1976

192 pp. 74 half-tones, 4 line drawings and 10 pp of maps.

Illustrated endpapers. 1976 to 1979. 2 OB jackets. A practical guide to archaeological sites in Britain with historical outline and gazetteer. About 46,000 sold.

First edition £5, others £3.

57.   Sewing by Meriel Tilling, 1975

192 pp. 8 colour plates, 44 half-tones and text diagrams by Barbara Firth. Illustrated endpapers. Single printing and jacket. 'A simple reference book for the home' for basic stitches, sewing techniques, mending and embroidery. About 42,000 sold. £4.

58.   Golf by Tom Scott, 1975

192 pp. 8 colour plates, 15 pp of half-tones and text drawings. 1975 to 1982. 3 OB jackets. An A to Z of golfing terms and personalities, with historical overview. New edition 1982. Small block print, deemed suitable for sports titles. About 75,000 sold.

First edition £5, others £2.

59.   Coarse Fishing by Peter Wheat, 1976

192 pp. 8 colour plates, 18 half-tones and numerous line drawings by Baz East. Photographic endpapers. 1976 to date. 2 OB jackets, NOB, PP (2 jackets), BB. Comprehensive guide to fishing know-how – fish, tackle, bait and methods. New edition 1984, revised 1989. A well-illustrated book, deservedly popular. About 100,000 sold to 1982.

First edition £4, others £2.

60.   Show Jumping and Eventing by Vivien Batchelor, 1976

192 pp. 44 line drawings by Christine Bousfield and 27 black & white photographs by Leslie Lane. Illustrated endpapers. 1976 to 1978. 2 OB jackets. Compendium of shows,

personalities, horses and competitions, with good drawings of courses and fences. New edition 1978. About 55,000 sold. £3.

61. Motorcycles by Robert M. Croucher, 1976

192 pp. Numerous black & white photographs. 1976 to date. 4 OB jackets, NOB, PP (3 jackets), BB. World's motorbikes arranged alphabetically by make. New editions 1977, 1980, 1982, 1984, 1986, 1988, 1991. The first edition, later improved, was micro-printed and barely readable. One of the most popular later titles, modelled on success of *Automobiles*. About 150,000 sold to 1981.

Elusive First edition £4, others £2.

62. Glass by Mary and Geoffrey Payton, 1976

192 pp. 8 colour plates and 95 half-tones. Single OB printing and jacket; reprinted BB. Companion to *Pottery and Porcelain* in similar A to Z format for 'those bitten by the collecting bug'. Half-tones better than average. About 30,000 sold. £4.

63. Tourist Atlas of Great Britain and Ireland, 1976

121 pp. Printed in colour throughout by John Bartholomew Ltd, Edinburgh. 1976 to 1981. 2 OB jackets. This was an unmodified Bartholomew pocket atlas bound as an Observer's book. About 62,000 sold. £4.

The Observer's Book of
SMALL CRAFT
GORDON FAIRLEY

64. Small Craft by Gordon Fairley, 1976

192 pp. 8 colour plates and over 260 half-tones and drawings by Brian Watson. Single printing and jacket. Compendium of sailing know-how and types of sailing craft (with a nod at power boats). About 80,000 sold. £4.

65. Tropical Fishes by Neil Wainwright, 1976

160 pp. 16 colour plates and 19 black & white drawings by Baz East. 1976 to date. 1 OB jacket, NOB, PP, BB. Describes 100 fish suitable for aquaria with notes on rearing and breeding. New format 1983. A popular title. About 61,000 to 1981.

First edition £5, others £2.

66. Farm Animals by Lawrence Alderson, 1976

192pp. 8 colour plates and black white photographs. 1976 to 1978. 1 OB jacket. Describes 100 breeds of sheep, cattle, farm horses, pigs, goats and poultry, along the lines of OB *Dogs* and *Horses and Ponies*. About 64,000 sold. £5.

67. Vegetables by Allan A. Jackson, 1977

°4 pp. 8 colour plates, 82 black

The Observer's Book of
VEGETABLES
ALLAN A. JACKSON

& white photographs and 5 diagrams. Illustrated endpapers. Single printing and jacket. Guide for home gardeners describing most available vegetables and herbs, with hints on cultivation. About 28,000 sold. Again, it *should* be quite scarce. £5.

68. Fly Fishing by Peter Wheat, 1977

192 pp. 8 colour plates, 23 half-tones and many line drawings by Baz East. Map endpapers. 1977 to date. 1 OB jacket, NOB, PP, BB. Companion to *Coarse Fishing* with know-how on flies, tackle, casting and fish. Revised 1980, 1984, 1989. About 45,000 to 1982.

First edition £7, others £3.

69. Coins by Howard Linecar, 1977

152 pp. Numerous half-tones and diagrams. Illustrated endpapers. 1977 to 1980. 2 OB jackets. Collector's guide to history and development of British coins. Retitled *British Coins* in 1980. Comprehensive, but shortweight compared with *Awards and Medals*. About 50,000 sold.

£4 in either version.

70. Seashells of the British Isles by Nora F. McMillan, 1977

158 pp. 8 colour plates by John Clegg and 195 line drawings by Bridget Finlow. Single printing and jacket. Describes the commoner British seashells with notes on habitats, life-histories, use and making a collection. About 30,000 sold. £4.

71. Fossils by Rhona M. Black, 1977

192 pp. 8 pp half-tone plates and 135 line drawings by the author. Illustrated endpapers. Single jacket and printing. Describes a selection of common animal and plant fossils with introduction on fossil environments and evolution. Colour would have helped. About 31,000 sold. £4.

72. Pets by Tina Hearne, 1978

192 pp. 8 colour plates, 31 half-tones and numerous line drawings by Christine Bousfield. 1978 to date. 1 OB jacket, NOB, PP, BB. Guide to the most popular children's pets with notes on care, rearing and habits. Revised 1978. Comprehensive but micro-printed. About 50,000 to 1981. £2.

73. The Cotswolds and Shakespeare Country by Geoffrey Palmer and Noel Lloyd, 1978

192 pp. 8 colour plates and 49 half-tones. Map endpapers. Single printing and jacket. An A to Z to villages and beauty spots in the Cotswolds and around Stratford-on-Avon. About 20,000 sold. Quite a scarce title. £10.

74. The Lake District by John Parker, 1978

192 pp. 8 colour plates and 67 half-tones. Single printing and jacket, but two version of map endpapers. A concise natural history and A to Z to England's largest National Park. About 38,000 sold. 'John Parker' was the pen name of former Park head ranger, John Wyatt. £6.

75.   Firearms by Nicholas du Quesne-Bird, 1978

The Observer's Book of
FIREARMS
NICHOLAS DU QUESNE-BIRD

192 pp. 119 half-tones and 9 line drawings. 1978. 1 OB jacket, reprinted BB. Describes history, development and collecting of hand-held guns, pistols, rifles and light machine-guns. About 50,000 sold. £3.

76.   Jazz by Mark White, 1978

192 pp. 76 half-tones. Photographic endpapers. Single printing and jacket. Enthusiast's jazz history, biography and 'discography'. About 20,000 sold. £5.

77.   Big Bands by Mark White, 1978

192 pp. 87 half-tones. Photographic endpapers. Single printing and jacket. Describes American, British and European dance bands, their music and their musicians. Companion to OB *Jazz,* and, like it, very readable, though it stretches the Observer's concept further than it was meant to go. About 20,000 sold. £5.

78.   Castles by Brian K. Davison, 1979

185 pp. 12 half-tones and 46 line drawings by Jasper Diamond. Map endpapers. 1979 to date. 1 OB jacket, NOB, PP, BB. Comprehensive guide to role, development and architectural elements of castles. 2nd edition (paperback) 1986. A fine book, arranged along the lines of *Cathedrals* and *Churches.*

First edition £5, others £2.

79. Caterpillars by David J. Carter, 1979

160 pp. 32 colour plates, line drawings and illustrated end-papers by Gordon Riley. Single printing and jacket. Describes and illustrates over 200 of the commoner and more conspicuous moth and butterfly larvae with notes on behaviour, food-plants, season and pupation. The most colourful book for many years. About 21,000 sold. Now rather scarce, and at least £5.

80. Rocks and Minerals by Frances and Richard Atkinson, 1979

184 pp. 58 colour and 7 half-tones; numerous line illustrations. 1 OB jacket; reprinted BB. Describes and illustrates 72 'common, economically important or interesting' minerals and 52 rock types from all over the world. The first new title to appear in laminated cover and also first to integrate colour printing with text. An attractive, well-illustrated book. About 23,000 sold. Rather scarce, £8.

81. Tennis by Clarence Jones, 1981

192 pp. 22 half-tones and text drawings. Single printing and jacket. Describes history, personalities and rules of the game along the lines of previous sports titles, but in commercial terms was the least successful. Print-run first year only about 8,000, yet not rare. £5.

82. Sea Fishing by Peter Wheat, 1980

190 pp. 8 colour plates, 14 half-tones and numerous drawings by Baz East. Photographic endpapers. A companion to *Coarse Fishing* and *Fly Fishing,* it describes fishing know-how on methods, tackle, tides and bait. Well written and illustrated, but the least popular of the three, and was only reprinted once. About 25,000 sold. Elusive. £10.

83. Devon and Cornwall, by Eric Delderfield, 1980
184 pp. 8 colour plates and 50 half-tones, mainly by author. Map endpapers. Single printing and jacket. An A to Z of the villages, houses and gardens, churches, museums and antiquities of the West Country. About 12,000 sold. £7.

Late rarities: Vintage Cars, Classic Cars, Herbs and Kitchen Antiques.

84.   Roses by Michael Gibson, 1980

192 pp. 130 colour photographs, many by author, and 12 line drawings. 1 OB jacket, reprinted BB. Comprehensive guide to rose growing, describing and illustrating 130 varieties. A colourful well illustrated book. About 18,000 sold. £7.

85.   Herbs by Mary Page, 1980

184 pp. 63 colour illustrations and 10 drawings by Norman Barber. 1 OB jacket; later revised as *The Gardener's Book of Herbs*. Describes and illustrates over 60 culinary and medicinal herbs with notes on cultivation and uses. About 15,000 sold, yet now one of the scarcest mainstream titles. £20.

86.   Never published. It was to have been **Country Houses.**

87.   Folk Song in Britain by Fred Woods, 1980

192 pp. 92 black & white photographs. Photographic endpapers. Single printing and jacket. Similar in treatment to *Jazz* and *Big Bands,* describes development of folk song, especially recent revival, followed by a Who's Who and discography. About 7,000 sold. £10.

88.   Silver by Elizabeth de Castres, 1980

186 pp. 96 half-tones and 18 line drawings. Single printing and jacket. An A to Z of silverware followed by guide to hallmarks. About 10,000 sold. £15.

89.   Tanks and other armoured vehicles by Charles Messenger, 1981

192 pp. 85 half-tones and 2-view silhouettes by Michael Badrocke. 1981 to date. 1 OB jacket, NOB, PP, BB. A reference guide to the world's armoured fighting vehicles,

with details of armament, crew, engine and role. New editions 1984, 1987. Arranged on similar lines to the Aircraft books. A popular title.

First edition £15, others £2.

90. Victoriana by Geoffrey Palmer and Noel Lloyd, 1981

192 pp. 8 colour plates and 87 half-tones. 1 OB jacket, reprinted BB. Practical guide for 'the collector with a limited purse but unlimited enthusiasm', describing the general state of arts and crafts in the Victorian era, followed by an A to Z. Well written book, though doomed to relatively low sales like many of the late titles – no more than 6,000 or so. Scarce. £20.

91. World Atlas, 1981

160 pp. Printed in colour throughout by John Bartholomew Ltd, Edinburgh. Single printing and jacket. This was an unmodified Bartholomew pocket atlas bound as an Observer's book, and is of slightly different dimensions to the rest of the series.

The scarcest of the later titles. A mint copy recently fetched £33 at auction.

92. Vintage Cars and pre-war classics by Mark White, 1982

184 pp. 8 colour plates and 45 half-tones. Single printing and jacket. Like *Classic Cars*, it has an ill-fitting laminated binding. An A to Z of pre-1939 cars arranged by make. Scarce. £15.

93. Classic Cars after 1945 by Mark White, 1982

184 pp. 8 colour plates and 49 half-tones. Single printing and jacket. Companion to *Vintage Cars* dealing with post-war thoroughbreds in a similar way. Very scarce. £20.

94. Paris by Elisabeth de Stroumillo, 1982

192 pp. 8 colour plates and 57 half-tones. Map endpapers. Single printing and jacket. Travel guide exploring history, ambience and key areas of Paris, along the lines of *London*. Scarce. £15.

95. Canals by John Gagg, 1982

192 pp. 8 colour plates, many half-tones by the author and drawings by Robert Wilson. 1982 to date. 1 OB jacket, PP, BB. Comprehensive guide to waterways, describing history, bridges and locks, canal users and today's network. New edition 1988. Well written and illustrated, one of the best recent titles. £10.

96. Gardens by Diana Saville, 1982

184 pp. 8 colour plates by author and 49 half-tones. Single printing and jacket. A guide to 140 public gardens in Britain with historical overview. A good subject for the series, constrained by lack of colour. £10.

97. Kitchen Antiques by John Woodforde, 1982

182 pp. Illustrated throughout with line drawings by Trevor Aldous. Single printing and jacket. Illustrates and describes over 230 antique household objects associated with kitchen, scullery or fireplace. Similar in layout to the author's OB *Furniture: a catalogue of bits and pieces*. Scarce. £25.

98. Opera by Elizabeth Forbes, 1982

192 pp. 16 pages of half-tones. Single printing and jacket. Describes the stories of the best known operas, listed by composer, A-Z, following short introduction on history of opera. Once regarded as one of the scarcest recent titles, but a cache of them was uncovered recently, apparently intended as free handouts at the Royal Albert Hall as a publicity stunt. Even so, they still cost £20.

The Observer's Pocket Series Collector's Society

The society was formed in 1991 with the intention of organising a newsletter and regular meetings for anyone interested in Observer's Books. The membership now stands at about 250, No. 22 of the society newsletter has recently been published, and innumerable 'swopmeets' have been held in different parts of the country and advertised in the newsletter. At the meetings you can sell, buy or exchange Observer's Books, enter the bidding at our informal auctions, or just pass the time of day with fellow enthusiasts, who (you may be relieved to know) are as normal as you!

Membership of the society costs £5 a year, for which you receive an average of four newsletters full of snippets and articles on the series and its fellow travellers. Cheques payable to OPSCS should be sent to the membership secretary, Alan Sledger, 10 Villiers Road, Kenilworth, Warwick CV8 2JB.

An Observer's bibliography, entitled *An Observer's look at Observer's Books,* contains all known English language hardback Observer's Books, as well as details of paperback issues, directories, Australian Observer's, Cyanamid jackets and other related publications. Almost all items are illustrated. The bibliography consists of 144 pages of photocopied information stored in clear plastic pages clipped into a ring-binder. It costs £22, plus £3.50 UK postage. Cheques with orders should be payable to the sole supplier, Mick Burgess at 139 Beatrice Road, Kettering, Northants NN16 9QR.

New Observer's Books

Certain titles in the series are now available under the Claremont Books imprint, part of Penguin Books Ltd.

Index

Figures in bold indicates an illustration.

184